Gardeners'
Worldmagazine

101 Garden Projects

10 9 8 7 6 5 4 3 2 1

Published in 2008 by BBC Books,
an imprint of Ebury Publishing
A Random House Group Company

Copyright © Woodlands Books Limited 2008
Edited by Helena Caldon
All photographs © *Gardeners' World Magazine*

The Random House Group Limited Reg. No. 954009

Addresses for companies within the Random House Group can be
found at www.randomhouse.co.uk

A CIP catalogue record for this book is available from the British Library.

The Random House Group Limited supports The Forest Stewardship
Council (FSC), the leading international forest certification organization.
All our titles that are printed on Greenpeace approved FSC certified
paper carry the FSC logo. Our paper procurement policy can be found
at www.rbooks.co.uk/environment

To buy books by your favourite authors and register for offers visit
www.rbooks.co.uk

Printed and bound by Firmengruppe APPL, aprinta druck,
Wemding, Germany
Colour origination by GRB Editrice Ltd., London

Commissioning Editor: Lorna Russell
Project Editor: Laura Higginson
Designer: Kathryn Gammon
Production: Bridget Fish

ISBN: 9781846074486

Gardeners'
World magazine

101 Garden Projects
QUICK AND EASY DIY IDEAS

Editor
Helena Caldon

Picture researcher
Janet Johnson

Contents

Introduction

It's easy to create a highly individual and pleasing garden with minimum effort and maximum inspiration. No matter how large or small your outdoor space, there are always simple jobs you can do that will make your garden pretty, practical or personal – whatever works for you.

So to give you all the inspiration you need, we've put together this selection of 101 simple, creative and useful projects for you to try. We think you'll be pleasantly surprised at just how much you can achieve – and we know you'll get a great sense of satisfaction into the bargain.

Simply flip through the pages and have a go at anything that inspires you. There are ideas for everyone, for all kinds of gardens and for all times of year, whether you want an easy project you can complete in just an hour or so on a summer evening after work, or a longer project you can get your teeth into on a winter day when you can't get outside. We're sure you'll find lots of ideas you won't be able to resist trying, so don't hold back – get out there and do something different today.

Helena Caldon
Gardeners' World Magazine

Revive old roses

You will need:
- Secateurs
- Gloves (optional)

When it comes to standard roses (plants with a single, long stem), you have to be cruel to be kind. It might seem brutal, but hard pruning will bring new life to an ageing rose bush and prevent the plant becoming top-heavy.

One of the keys to success is timing – you should make the cuts in winter when the plant is dormant. Armed with a sharp, clean pair of secateurs, look out for any damaged, diseased, dead or spindly shoots on the plant and remove these completely. Then trim all the remaining stems back to about 20cm (8in) long to create a tidy and well-balanced, rounded shape. Also carefully snip off any young shoots that are sprouting from the single main stem of standard roses.

TIP
To prevent the spread of infection, dispose of any diseased shoots or leaves that you remove from the plant, as well as any debris around its base.

Warm up winter beds

When to do it: January–March

You will need:

- Polythene sheeting or old carpet
- Planks or bricks

In the depths of winter, don't stare mournfully at empty veg beds while you flick through seed catalogues and plan next year's harvest – warm up your soil and you can be sowing seeds all the sooner.

Warming your soil allows you to get ahead and prepare your beds on frosty spring days when everyone else is waiting for their soil to defrost (working soil while it's frozen will destroy its structure).

The easiest way to warm up soil is simply to tuck it up for the winter. Before you do this, you need to fork over the soil, rake it and level it, and then you can cover it with a large sheet of polythene. Tuck the edges of the sheeting tight to the sides of your beds and bury them, or hold them down with planks or plenty of bricks.

Covering cold, bare soil in this way not only keeps it toasty for spring, but also has the bonus of preventing pesky weeds getting a foothold over the winter and early spring.

TIP
Pieces of old carpet work just as well as polythene, and as they're usually quite heavy they need less weighting down.

Re-pot an agapanthus

When to do it: February–June

You will need:

■ Agapanthus plant

■ Pot – just a little larger than the pot it's in already

■ Crocks (broken pieces of terracotta pot) or pebbles

■ Loam-based compost

Agapanthus is one of many plants that flowers best when its roots are quite tightly packed into its pot. However, it's still worth repotting the plant once a year to give it fresh compost to root into, along with the nutrients it needs for new growth.

Choose a container that has holes in its base and is only a little larger than the pot the plant is already in, or one that's just large enough for its roots. Put crocks or pebbles in the base of the new pot to ensure good drainage, then add enough compost so that the top of the plant's rootball ends up slightly below the rim of the new pot when positioned inside.

Knock the agapanthus out of its current pot, lightly firm down the compost in the base of the new pot, then set the plant in position. Fill the gap between the rootball and the sides of the new pot with more compost, adding it gradually and pushing it down with your fingers as you go. Continue adding compost to the pot until it's level with the top of the rootball, then water the plant thoroughly.

TIP
Use a loam-based John Innes No. 2 compost when repotting as this will provide more nutrients than a multi-purpose type.

Boost your lawn

When to do it: spring or autumn

You will need:

- Rake
- Grass seed or turf
- Compost
- Watering can or hose
- Pegs and netting or clear polythene
- Spade

After a long, wet winter, your lawn might be looking a little sad, and a thorough raking could reveal bare patches where the grass is undernourished or where it's been worn away altogether. Sowing seed in these patches in early spring gives the lawn a chance to get going so it'll be strong enough to cope with the summer's wear and tear. Filling the gaps at this time of year will also prevent moss and weeds moving in before the grass can naturally spread.

Rake over the bare patch to loosen the soil surface, then sprinkle on an appropriate lawn seed mix, scattering half the seeds in one direction and the rest in the other to give an even distribution. Thinly cover the area with compost and then water it. Protect the newly sown seed from hungry birds by pegging netting or clear polythene over it.

A more expensive but instant solution is to use turf. Simply dig out a shallow square slightly larger than the bare patch, rake the soil and add a little topsoil if needed, then patch the gap with a new piece of turf, cut to fit.

TIP
A small sheet of polythene pegged over the seeds will encourage them to germinate, but it'll also keep the rain off, so you'll need to water regularly.

Lay new turf

When to do it: March–April or September–October

You will need:
- Spade
- Wheelbarrow
- Topsoil
- Rake
- Turf
- Scaffolding plank
- Sharp knife
- Watering can or hosepipe

If your lawn is looking a little the worse for wear, the simplest remedy is to lay new turf. It's more expensive than sowing seed, but you do get an instant lawn.

Before your new turf is delivered, prepare the area carefully. Level the ground and remove any large stones. If the surface is uneven, wheelbarrow in some topsoil, pour it on and even it out with a rake. Firm the soil surface by walking up and down on it, taking small, shuffling steps. Fill any dips with more topsoil and compress it again with your feet. Give the surface a final rake over. Get all of this done before your turf arrives, so you can lay it straight away and not leave it to dry out.

Lay the turves one by one on to the prepared soil, butting each strip together as tightly as possible and staggering the joints like brickwork. Do avoid walking directly on the new turf – work from a plank placed across it instead. Trim any awkward shapes right at the end, cutting off the excess turf with a sharp knife. Bang the turves down with the back of a rake so they make good contact with the soil, then give the whole area a good watering. Your lawn will establish in a few weeks – water it regularly during this time so the turves don't dry out. Start mowing when the grass is 12–15cm (4½–6in) high.

TIP
Lay a new lawn or patch up an old one during a warm spring or autumn – rain helps the grass establish roots in time for summer sun or winter frosts.

Spring clean your paths, paving and patio

When to do it: March–September

You will need:
- Broom
- Patio cleaner and stiff brush – or pressure washer
- Trowel
- Path weedkiller (optional)

Grime, slime and moss accumulate on most paths, patios, steps and decking during the winter months, making the surfaces grubby, not to mention slippery. Get outside and give your hard surfaces a spring clean.

Using a broom, sweep away any debris and the worst of the muck from paved or decked areas. Then remove any stubborn marks or dirt on the paving using a special patio cleaner and a stiff brush, or invest in a pressure washer for a less labour-intensive job. These washers just need to be connected to a mains power source and an outdoor tap, and can be bought quite cheaply or you can hire one.

Use an old trowel to scrape out any moss or weeds growing between slabs or brick paviours for a clean finish. Occasional applications of a path weedkiller to the area once you have cleared it will prevent new weeds developing.

TIP
Always use pressure washers carefully, as their powerful jets can erode the surface of some types of paving.

Revive your ferns

When to do it: April–May

You will need:
- Secateurs
- Composted bark mulch

As spring and brighter days arrive, most deciduous ferns are looking rather the worse for wear and need a little tender loving care to rouse them from their winter slumber. Now's the time to get busy with a pair of secateurs, before the ferns burst forth with new growth.

Trim off all the old, brown, tattered-looking leaves to expose the new fronds emerging beneath and to give them space to unfurl. Once you've trimmed away all the dead and damaged leaves, spread a mulch of composted bark around the plants to nourish the soil and help it retain moisture.

TIP
Trim away the old fronds while the new ones are still tightly curled, as it's easier to get to the base of the old leaves.

Make plants for free

You will need:

- Two forks
- Spade or sharp knife (optional)
- Trowel
- Garden compost

As spring arrives, many perennials wake up from their winter sleep and begin to romp away with renewed vigour. However, some plants might need a helping hand to rejuvenate them and get them back into peak condition. Dividing perennials gives them a new lease of life, allowing them to produce lots of fresh growth – and you get new plants into the bargain to put in other parts of the garden or share with friends.

Most perennials should be divided in spring, before growth really gets going. Use a fork to lift the plant and its roots from the border and place it on the ground. Divide the plant by prising the roots apart with two forks set back to back or, if the roots are really congested, use a sharp knife or spade to slice through them.

Discard any old, weak or woody growth (usually in the centre of the clump) and keep only the healthy portions. Then you can replant the divisions, preferably in groups of three or five for a bold, well-balanced display. Dig out each of the new planting holes with a trowel, then fork plenty of garden compost into the base.

TIP
Make sure there are at least two growth buds or shoots on each section that you replant.

Encourage fuchsia flowers

When to do it: April–June

You will need:
- Sharp, fine-pointed scissors or knife (optional)

Fuchsias bring an elegant splash of colour to a border or patio container, and with a little coaxing you can have a vast troupe of summer flowers dancing over just one shapely plant.

All you need to do is regularly pinch out the plant's soft growing tips to encourage the development of bushy sideshoots, and more shoots means more flowers. For the best display, start pinching out in spring and continue until early summer. The first flowers will be produced around four to six weeks after the last pinch.

With young fuchsia plants or rooted cuttings, pinch out the soft shoot tips after two to three pairs of leaves have been produced, using scissors, a knife or your fingernails. Repeat the pinching two or three more times, allowing two pairs of leaves to expand fully on each of the subsequent sideshoots. This process may take between 10 and 20 days, depending on the speed of growth.

TIP
Pinching out the tips of hardy garden fuchsias stops the plants becoming leggy, and will ensure masses of blooms from summer into autumn.

Show your support

You will need:
- Pea sticks, bamboo canes, tripods or plant supports
- Soft string or plant ties

There's nothing more dispiriting than the sight of majestic herbaceous plants and perennials flopping and sagging when they should be towering proudly above their neighbours and unfurling dramatic blooms. In a British summer this is all too often the case, as strong winds or heavy rains in June can batter delphiniums and other lofty border gems before they have a chance to flower.

Particularly in inclement summers, many such plants need a helping hand to prevent them flopping on to their neighbours or over the edges of lawns and paths. And the key to success is to put the plant supports in place early – this not only ensures the plants stay upright from the start, but also means that even the most obvious structures will soon be hidden from view, as foliage will grow to cover them in just a few weeks.

Spiral stakes pushed into the ground alongside the base of the plant's stem are perfect for this purpose, as you can gently wind shoot tips around them as they grow.

TIP
Bamboo canes will do the job just as well. Tie the tall stems of delphiniums or dahlias individually to canes pushed into the soil alongside the developing shoots. Secure with soft string at 10–15cm (4-6in) intervals up the stems.

Trim your hedges

When to do it: May–August

You will need:
- Electric or petrol-powered hedge-trimmer
- Safety goggles and gloves
- String line and canes
- Secure ladder and/or work platform for tall hedges

As your garden wakes up in spring and all the plants in your borders burst into new growth, it's time to trim the hedges while you can still get to them.

The easiest way to achieve a slick, regular and even finish is to trim established conifer or small-leaved hedges using a powered hedge-trimmer. To provide a straight cutting line, push bamboo canes vertically down through the hedge at regular intervals, and run taut string between them marking the top edge of the hedge.

Trim the hedge top by holding the hedge-trimmer horizontally with both hands and use the string line as a guide. Wear protective goggles and gloves, and if cutting a tall hedge make sure you have a firm footing on a stable ladder. Clip the sides using the string as a guide again. Hold the hedge-trimmer vertically and make long, sweeping strokes to ensure an even finish. Remove the canes and string line before using the hedge-trimmer to tidy up the top edges. Hold the cutting bar at a 45-degree angle.

It's a satisfying job and one that should only need doing a couple of times a year, although quick-growing conifers often need three cuts during the growing season, at roughly eight-week intervals.

TIP
Trim large-leaved hedging plants, such as laurel, with shears and secateurs, taking care not to cut the leaves in half – if you do so they'll go brown at the cut edges, making the hedge look tatty.

Prune your way to perfect wisteria

When to do it: late June – August, mid-October – March

You will need:

- Secateurs
- String for tying in (optional)
- Ladder (optional)

There are few sights as spectacular as a gnarled wisteria dripping with blooms in late spring, adorning the facade of a house from roof to ground, or smothering a pergola or archway. But to get such a breathtaking flowering display, you need to devote just a little time to your plant twice a year. Pruning in summer and again in winter encourages the development of the short, flowering spurs that will carry the blooms in spring.

In summer, any time from late June onwards, cut back all the long, vigorous shoots that have been produced in spring and early summer to just beyond the second or third bud from the base. If you're initially training a young plant, select a few strong shoots to tie into wires or trellis and then, in future years, you can prune sideshoots back to this framework.

From mid-October onwards, prune recent growth back to two or three buds from the base again. Cut with secateurs just above the chosen bud, at an angle slanting slightly away from the bud, so rainwater won't run down on to it.

TIP

Make sure your secateurs are sharp when cutting back the long shoots of climbers, as it's easy to crush or tear the stems, which may lead to die-back.

Tidy up your lavender

When to do it: July–August

You will need:

■ Secateurs or shears

Whether you have a few lavender plants dotted around your garden or an informal lavender hedge, you'll prolong the life and flowering of these plants if you give them a good trim once the blooms have faded.

Simply remove the faded flowering stems, cutting back into the current season's shoots, to create a neatly rounded bush. Be careful not to cut into the old, woody stems because new shoots won't grow from there and you'll be left with bare patches. When trimming individual plants, it's best to use a pair of secateurs, but if you're clipping a whole hedge you'll make lighter work of the job with a pair of shears.

When trimming an informal lavender hedge, shape it gently by eye as you go. But for a more formal result, use a taut line of string set to the top and sides of the hedge in order to get a straight, level cut.

TIP

If you want the lavender flowers for potpourri, cut them before they open fully, as their aromatic oils quickly evaporate on warm days.

Make luscious leaf mould

When to do it: September–November

You will need:

- Weed-suppressing membrane
- 4 wooden posts
- Rubber mallet (or trowel/small spade)
- 4.5m (3½ft) length of galvanised chicken wire
- Pliers and garden wire
- Flat-tined rake or electric leaf blower

If the sight of falling leaves makes you think only of the mess and clearing up involved, try looking at it as a golden opportunity to produce a free supply of mulch, soil improver and potting medium, all in one! Making luscious leaf mould is like gardening alchemy, turning dull leftovers into a rich prize – and it's really easy to do.

To build a composting cage, simply cover the ground with weed-suppressing membrane and, using a rubber mallet, hammer four posts into the ground 1m apart to form a square (if your soil is too hard, dig holes for the posts instead). Wrap chicken wire around the outside of the posts and secure the ends together with garden wire. Then collect up your leaves – either give yourself some exercise and use a flat-tined rake, or make life easier and hire or buy an electric leaf blower. Deposit the leaves in their new home and let nature do the rest.

Alternatively, if you only have a small quantity of leaves, place them in a plastic bag spiked with holes, add a little water and tie the top, then leave for a year or two to rot down.

TIP
The leaves of deciduous trees rot down quite quickly, but evergreen leaves and conifer needles take far longer, so don't add too many unless you're prepared to wait.

Protect tender plants outside

When to do it: October

You will need:
- Horticultural fleece or hessian
- String
- Straw and chicken wire

With milder winters becoming more common, tender exotics are popular additions to gardens as they now stand a fair chance of survival in a sheltered spot. However, even in mild areas you may still get some sub-zero temperatures and the occasional frost, so to save tears in spring, err on the side of caution and wrap up your delicate plants before winter sets in. Plants such as half-hardy tree ferns, bananas, palms, cannas, ginger lilies and echiums are all candidates for winter protection.

With banana plants and tree ferns, tie horticultural fleece or hessian around the foliage and trunk, securing it with string. Both materials let in light, air and water but also provide insulation. With more vulnerable plants, make a sturdy cage of chicken wire around them and pack it with straw (see picture). Protect tender tubers, such as those of dahlias and cannas, by spreading a generous layer of mulch over the surface of the soil.

TIP
If you're concerned about any tender plants, lift them and bring them indoors over winter, returning them to the garden once all danger of frost has passed.

Improve your soil

When to do it: October–March

You will need:
- Spade
- Fork
- Compost or well-rotted manure
- Fertiliser
- Rake

Happy, healthy plants give the best results, and fertilisers are a quick-fix way to give your plants a boost throughout the growing season. But to get flowers and crops off to the best possible start, it's worth adding nutrients before you plant. Improving the soil with plenty of organic matter aids drainage and aeration on heavy soils and helps to retain essential moisture on light soils.

Before you add the organic matter, dig over the soil thoroughly using a spade and fork to break up large clods. Remove any weeds and debris as you go. Spread a minimum 5cm (2in) layer of home-made garden compost, bagged compost or well-rotted manure over the surface, then dig it in, mixing it with the soil to the depth of the spade or fork tines.

Tread the area, using your heels to firm the soil. Break up any remaining large lumps with the back of your fork. And finally, sprinkle fertiliser over the surface at the rate recommended on the packet, then use a rake to mix it into the soil and to create a level surface for planting or sowing.

TIP

In areas already planted with bulbs or perennials, simply spread the organic matter over the soil surface in autumn and let the worms take it down into the ground during winter.

Share your apple harvest

You will need:
- 1m (3½ft) length of 2mm (⅛in) galvanised wire
- Pencil
- Skewer
- Apples (approx 10)
- Pliers
- Garden string

As you cut back your plants in autumn and watch the squirrels plundering what they can from your garden, spare a thought for the birds that might visit over winter and leave them a little snack to keep them coming. These beautiful apple wreaths are loved by birds, which feast on the fruits as they rot, and they're quick and easy to make.

Take your piece of wire, bend it in half and twist it together. Ask a friend to hold the two loose ends, then, using a pencil in the loop for leverage, twist the wire. Poke a hole through the apples (from top to bottom) using the skewer. Thread the twisted wire through the apples, loose ends first. Once the wire is full, guide the loose ends through the loop at the other end to form a circle, then hook the loose ends over with pliers to secure in place. Hang up the wreath with a piece of string, using it to cover any exposed wire where the metal joins at the top.

TIP
You can replenish the wreath with more apples as they get eaten, or have a replacement wreath ready and waiting.

Sow sweet peas for summer scent

When to do it: October–June

You will need:
- Sweet pea seeds
- Pots
- Potting compost
- Horticultural grit
- Clear polythene bags and rubber bands
- Bamboo canes, wigwams or trellis
- Garden twine

Nothing can beat the delicate fragrance of sweet peas drifting across the garden on a warm summer's day – the sight of their fragile flowers clambering up canes, trellis, wigwams or even other plants lets you know that sunny days are here. And thanks to their prolific and long-lasting flowering habit, you can be sure of pretty, perfumed cut flowers for several months. All they need is a sunny spot in your garden and they'll happily scramble away all summer long, with just a little help from you.

Sweet peas are best sown indoors in mid-autumn – the soil outdoors is too cold for sowing until April. Plant the seeds in pots filled with compost mixed with a little horticultural grit to aid drainage. Secure clear polythene bags over the pots until the seedlings appear, then remove them. Give the seedlings plenty of light, and once they've developed three or four pairs of leaves, pinch out the growing tip to encourage sideshoots to form.

In mid-spring, harden off your young sweet peas, then plant them in the garden at the base of canes, wigwams or trellis. Tie the stems to their supports as they grow, pinching out the weaker shoots until the main stem is well established.

TIP
You can also sow sweet pea seeds in spring, and you'll have sensational flowers a little later in the summer.

Prepare for a bean feast

When to do it: November–February

You will need:
- Spade
- Kitchen waste or compostable material

If your compost bin is full but not ready to empty yet, make a composting trench to feed next year's vegetable crop. It's a great way to enrich the soil and increase its capacity to hold water – and your beans will love it!

Simply choose where you want to grow your beans next year – in your veg beds, borders or another space in the garden that you've set aside – and dig a trench about 23cm (9in) deep. Add a generous 8cm (3½in) layer of kitchen waste to the bottom of the trench, then return all the soil back into the trench and leave it over winter. The kitchen waste will gradually rot down and, by the time you're all set to plant out your beans, there will be a feast of nutrients ready and waiting to give them a real kick-start.

TIP
Used tea bags, vegetable and fruit peelings and eggshells are ideal kitchen waste for composting, but don't add any cooked food or you could encourage mice and other vermin.

Tools overhaul

When to do it: November–February

You will need:

- Garden tools
- Bucket of sand
- Kitchen foil
- Old pots
- Bucket of hot water with sterilising fluid

After a summer of activity, most garden sheds are in a bit of a cluttered, disorganised mess come autumn. So before you pack everything away for the winter, and while there's not much gardening to be done, take the opportunity to give your tools a good clean and to tidy up your shed.

Don't put your tools away for the winter if they're still mucky – they need a quick clean. With metal tools, such as spades, forks and trowels, drive them into a bucket of sand to remove any hint of dirt, grass and mud. Then scrunch up a ball of kitchen foil and buff the metal surfaces. It'll bring up a shine and is also great for removing rust.

Next, gather up all your old pots and clean them thoroughly – scrub them with a brush in hot water containing added sterilising agent, such as Jeyes Fluid, so they're ready for use next spring.

And finally, organise your tools and kit so they're all easily accessible – you should be able to get to everything, even when the shed is full of overwintering garden chairs and parasols.

TIP
If you haven't got enough storage space, try making a tool rack (page 104) to keep things tidy and out of the way.

Install a water butt

When to do it: set it up in autumn, use it all year

You will need:
- Water butt
- Connector kit (usually comes with the water butt)
- Water butt stand or bricks

If there's the possibility of a hosepipe ban in your area, don't despair – install a water butt and you can save precious rainwater whenever it falls, which should keep your plants happy through a dry spell. Water butts are inexpensive, and what you do spend pays dividends for the environment and can even cut your bills if your water is metered.

Water butts come in a range of different sizes and shapes, from slim-line models to enormous tanks, to suit gardens large and small. They can be attached to a downpipe from the guttering on your house, shed or greenhouse. If you're really keen and have lots of suitable space, you can even buy several butts and link them together to collect more water from a single source.

When attaching your water butt to a downpipe, take time before you cut into the pipe to set the butt up on its stand, or on some bricks, so you can make sure the tap is at the right height for your watering can. Water butts are simple to install – they should come with full instructions, along with a connector kit. And once you've got yours in position, you can just sit back and wait for the rain to do the rest.

TIP
Remove fallen leaves from the guttering regularly through autumn and winter – this will ensure rainwater doesn't overflow and get wasted, and will keep debris out of your water butt.

Extend the bulb season

You will need:
- One or more large pots
- Several aquatic baskets to fit inside each pot
- Selection of spring bulbs for a long-flowering season
- Multi-purpose compost

If you want your spring bulb display to go on a little longer, try this simple way to perk up your pots as the flowers fade.

Buy one or more ornamental pots and several aquatic baskets for each, making sure they fit comfortably inside – we planted up four different baskets per pot to provide colour from February to June.

Add compost to the baskets to an appropriate level for the planting depth required for your bulbs. Plant one basket with dwarf irises or crocuses (to flower in February/March), another with daffodils (to follow in March), a third with late-flowering tulips (for April/May) and a fourth with Dutch irises (for June). Keep the baskets well watered and place in a sheltered spot to develop.

When the flowers of the first basket are starting to form, simply drop it into one of the ornamental pots, and swap over as each display fades.

TIP
The rule of thumb when planting bulbs is to plant them at twice to three times the length of the bulb.

Take root cuttings

You will need:
- Fork
- Sharp knife
- Large pots
- Gritty compost mix made from equal parts grit or perlite and potting compost
- Label and pencil

If you're spending your winter evenings planning your garden for next year and thinking about all the gaps in your beds and borders that need filling, then before you head down to the garden centre, see if there are any of your existing perennials that you could propagate from.

Winter is the perfect time to take root cuttings to increase your stocks of perennials, such as phlox, mint, Japanese anemones and primulas. It couldn't be easier to do, and by spring you'll be potting up your new plants.

Choose the plant you'd like to take cuttings from and gently lift the whole clump out of the ground using a fork, taking care not to damage the roots. Wash the roots to remove some of the soil. Then, with a sharp knife, cut off several 5cm (2in) lengths of healthy root. When you have enough cuttings, replant the parent plant. Next, fill some pots with gritty compost and lay the root cuttings, well spaced apart, on the surface. Cover the cuttings with a thin layer of compost, water well, label the pots, and place them in a cool spot indoors or outside in a cold-frame.

TIP
Thick roots can be pushed vertically into planting holes made with a pencil, but make sure they go in the right way up – roots will form at the end that was furthest away from the parent plant.

Sow green manure

When to do it: all year round

You will need:
- Seeds for green manure, depending on the season

If your crops are harvested, it's time to think about preparing the soil for the next lot. Rather than forking in well-rotted manure or compost grow a green manure. It enriches and breaks up the soil, needing only a minimal amount of digging.

Green manures are plants sown directly into bare ground purely to be dug back into the soil in order to improve its fertility and boost the organic content. They also keep weeds at bay on an empty plot by covering the soil so they can't grow.

You can leave green manures in place for anything up to a year if you wish, but most gardeners don't have the luxury of that much space. It's usually best to opt for a crop that is sown and grown in just six weeks. If you need a quick fix in summer, sow buckwheat, mustard, phacelia or fenugreek; in the winter months grow winter tares or Italian ryegrass (though this needs a little more digging in than other green manures).

It's important not to let the plants flower, and if they look like they're about to, simply chop off the tops. When you're ready to use the bed again, cut the plants down to the ground, leave for a day or two, then dig them back into the soil.

TIP
If you do have an area of ground that you won't be cultivating for a year, then sow a long-term manure, such as winter beans, red clover or alfalfa. Chop the plants back occasionally to keep them under control until you're ready to dig them in.

Plant shallots

When to do it: February–March

You will need:
- Shallot bulbs
- Trowel
- Fork

Shallots are one of the earliest crops you can plant outside in the new year, and are well worth growing if you love tasty food as they have a delicious, slightly milder flavour than onions.

Growing your own shallots couldn't be easier. In February or March, plant the small bulbs (or sets), which are available from mail-order suppliers and many garden centres, straight into prepared ground. Space them 15cm (6in) apart, in rows about 20cm (8in) apart, to give them room to grow and allow you to easily hoe out any weeds that grow between them.

Place each bulb with its tip hidden just below soil level. All you need to do now is keep them weed free and well watered in dry spells, and your crop of shallots will be ready to harvest in July or August, when the leaves turn yellow naturally. Lift the clumps with a fork, taking care not to damage the bulbs, and dry them off in the sun if you're going to store them.

TIP
Before planting, trim off any dry, wispy tops to prevent birds using them to tug the shallots out of the ground, or cover them with netting until they get established.

Get a head start on strawberries

When to do it: March–April

You will need:

■ 3 strawberry plants (pot grown or lifted from the garden)
■ Large pot or hanging basket
■ Multi-purpose compost

For many people, strawberries say summer. While you can't make the sun come out any earlier, you can get strawberries a good four to six weeks ahead of outdoor plants – as early as late April if you plant the right varieties, like 'Royal Sovereign' or 'Cambridge Favourite'.

Potted up in March and brought into a cool greenhouse or conservatory, strawberry plants will quickly come into growth and start to flower and fruit. The key is to keep them well lit, well ventilated and well watered to prevent the plants becoming leggy and drawn.

Put two or three strawberry plants into a large pot or hanging basket filled with multi-purpose compost. You can get the plants from beds outdoors or use pot-grown ones – both will be happy indoors. Water the plants regularly and open the greenhouse vents or conservatory windows on warm days. As the fruit begins to develop, cut off any long runners that the plants throw out as these will divert energy from the crop.

If you're growing the strawberries in a pot on the ground, check the plants carefully as the fruit develops for signs of slug damage. It might also be worth netting the plants, or even the greenhouse doors and vents, to stop birds stealing the fruit as it ripens.

TIP
In very hot weather, shade strawberry plants growing under glass with fine netting or horticultural fleece to stop them getting scorched.

Prepare for pots of potatoes

When to do it: March–April

You will need:

■ Large pot or potato barrel

■ Crocks (pieces of broken terracotta pot) or large stones

■ Multi-purpose compost

■ Seed potatoes (already chitted)

If you have a small garden, or just a small veg bed, you don't have to sacrifice precious soil space to produce your own potatoes – a sizable container is all you need. You can buy a potato barrel in many garden centres or online, but you can just as well grow potatoes in a large pot that's at least 30cm (12in) deep and wide. If you can get hold of a 45cm (18in) pot, then you can plant up to three tubers in it.

To crop well, potatoes need good drainage, so put a layer of crocks or stones into the bottom of the container before half-filling it with multi-purpose compost. Place each tuber into the compost with its 'eyes', or sprouts, facing upwards and cover with a few centimetres of compost. Water well, and keep the compost moist at all times.

When the first shoots appear, pile more compost on top (a process known as earthing up). The potatoes are ready for harvesting when the flowers start to open – usually around June or July. Simply tip the pot up and collect your potatoes.

TIP

An even easier way to grow potatoes is to plant them in a large bag of compost. Sit the bag up vertically, open it at one end and plunge a couple of seed potatoes deep inside, ensuring there's a minimum of 10cm (4in) of compost covering the tubers. If any push to the surface as they grow, add more compost.

Make every day a salad day

When to do it: March–August

You will need:
- Salad seeds
- Modular trays and compost (optional)

If your bag of supermarket salad in the fridge seems to disappear faster than you can replace it, why not grow your own to keep up with demand? If you sow little and often, you can keep the leaves coming right through to autumn.

Salads are one of the speediest crops you can grow, but to ensure there's more ready and waiting when you finish picking your first batch, you need to look ahead and sow at regular intervals. If you don't have enough space in your veg bed to have several rows growing at different stages, then sow the seed into modular trays filled with compost. Keep these to one side or under cover, then plant out the seedlings into the beds as gaps occur.

TIP
If life is hectic and repeat sowing times seem to pass you by, mark a reminder to yourself on your calendar, say, on the first Saturday of every month.

Sow easy peas in guttering

When to do it: March–May

You will need:

- Lengths of plastic guttering
- Fine-tooth tenon saw or hacksaw
- Multi-purpose compost
- Pea seeds
- Watering can

If you have trouble with pea or mangetout crops when sowing outdoors, one solution is to start them off indoors instead. Sowing them in pots, though, means you're faced with having to transplant the delicate young plants with as little disturbance as possible when the time comes to plant them out. Natural-fibre pots, which degrade in the soil, can help avoid this, but sowing the seed into guttering is a guaranteed, hassle-free method.

Arm yourself with some cheap plastic guttering and, using a saw, trim it into lengths that measure the same as the width of your vegetable bed. Fill each section with compost, stopping just short of the ends, and firm it down gently so it's level with the rim. Space your seeds evenly along the length of the guttering,

about 2.5cm (1in) apart, in two rows, then push the seeds about 1cm down. Cover the seeds, then place the guttering in an unheated greenhouse. If you don't let the compost dry out, the seeds should germinate in about a week.

When the seedlings are ready to plant out, dig a shallow trench across your vegetable bed to the depth of the guttering and slide the row of plants out of the guttering and straight into their new home. Water the plants in well, and push in canes next to them; tie the stems to the canes as the plants grow.

TIP

This method of scwing is good for many other crops too (except root crops), and is particularly effective when sowing salads in succession.

Raise your own watercress

When to do it: April–September

You will need:
- Small and large pots
- Multi-purpose compost
- Watercress seeds (a good variety is 'Aqua', which is available from seed suppliers)
- Watering can

Contrary to popular belief, you don't need a stream or pond in your garden to be able to grow watercress – all you need are a few pots that are kept well watered and you can be cropping the cress for salads, soups and sandwiches all summer.

To grow your own watercress, fill some small pots with multi-purpose compost, sprinkle over the seeds and water well. The seeds should germinate in a couple of weeks. Keep watering them during this time and place in good light. Once they've formed good root systems, divide the young plants and move small clumps into larger pots.

Water these pots regularly and keep a close check on them to ensure they are damp at all times. In four to six weeks the watercress is ready to harvest, and you can continue picking from the plants for several months.

TIP
Regular harvesting encourages the plants to carry on producing fresh leaves, so keep picking.

Steal a march on runner beans

When to do it: late May–mid-June

You will need:

- Runner bean seeds or young plants
- Spade
- Garden compost or well-rotted manure
- Long bamboo canes or sticks
- Garden twine
- Trowel

Runner beans may not have the sophisticated appeal of French beans, but they're as reliable and heavy cropping as they are tasty, and they're worthy of a place in any veg garden. Early summer is the perfect time to plant runner beans. Get them going in May or June and they'll thrive in the warm, moist soil, quickly scrambling up their supports.

Before planting, give the young bean seedlings a thorough watering. Meanwhile, tie some long bamboo canes or sticks together to form a wigwam, over an area of soil that has been improved by digging in plenty of garden compost or well-rotted manure. Using a trowel, dig a hole at the base of each cane and put in one plant, making sure the top of the rootball is level with the surrounding soil.

Fill in around the roots with soil and firm down gently with your fingers.

Water the plants well, then add a 5cm (2in) deep mulch of damp compost around the base of the plants to help retain moisture in the soil. Coax the bean stems to climb by carefully twining them around the canes as they grow. Once the beans start cropping, keep picking to encourage more.

TIP

If you didn't sow seeds indoors in April, you can sow outdoors at the end of April or in early May. If you've left sowing too late, you can buy young plants instead.

Raising super-fresh salads

When to do it: May–September

You will need:

- Bread bin, colander, large pot or other quirky containers
- Loam-based potting compost
- Fine composted bark
- Crocks or stones
- Purple shiso (*Perilla frutescens* var. *purpurescens*)
- Thai basil (*Ocimum basilicum* 'Horapha Nanum')
- Pot marigolds (*Calendula officinalis*)
- Red lettuce 'Rusty'
- Radishes, mixed seeds

There's nothing nicer on a warm, summer evening than a fresh, full-flavoured salad on the dinner table – except, that is, a delicious, home-grown salad that you've picked seconds earlier from just outside your kitchen door.

All the herbs used in this arrangement are annuals, needing to be sown fresh every year, so they're best grown in pots to avoid bare beds from autumn to spring. We sowed purple shiso and Thai basil in a large terracotta pot to give them plenty of room to grow. In front of this we planted red lettuces in a traditional enamel bread bin, along with edible marigold flowers, and sowed radishes in a colander.

These herbs don't like full sun as the compost will dry out too quickly, so ideally the containers should be positioned in partial shade. Plant all the herbs in a mix of three parts multi-purpose compost to one part fine composted bark to provide good drainage, and put crocks into the bottom of each pot before filling with compost.

TIP
You can use any type of container for herbs, provided you fill it with the free-draining compost they need. Punch plenty of drainage holes into the base of the pot if it doesn't already have any.

Prepare for a brew When to do it: May–September

You will need:

■ Teapots, mugs, cups, bowls, jugs
■ Herbs for brewing – lemon verbena (*Aloysia triphylla*), chamomile (*Chamaemelum nobile*), mint, lemon balm (*Melissa officinalis*), hyssop, thyme

If you like to keep your herbs close at hand for a really fresh brew, why not grow some in fun, tea-themed containers in your kitchen? Using teapots, jugs, mugs and cups is a convenient and attractive way of growing herbs that need to be in full view.

What you grow is up to you: lemon balm will perk you up if you're feeling tired, and is said to relieve headaches and tension, and restore memory. Lemon verbena has relaxing properties and is particularly refreshing as an iced tea on a hot summer day. Mint is the old favourite for aiding digestion, and when mixed with hyssop it's a delicious tea to soothe an irritating cough. Thyme is an antiseptic, good for mouthwashes and even hangovers!

When you want a brew, simply put a handful of fresh herbs into a mug, pour over boiling water and leave to infuse for five minutes. Keep it covered as the steam contains the beneficial essential oils.

TIP
Sow or plant the herbs in standard plastic pots that can be dropped into and lifted out of the containers easily.
You can start off with potted herbs from the supermarket while you wait for your sowings to grow.

The herb family's Famous Five

When to do it: May–September

You will need:
- Five pots (3 large, 2 smaller ones)
- Crocks (broken terracotta pots) or stones
- Loam-based potting compost
- Multi-purpose compost
- Rosemary (*Rosmarinus officinalis* 'Boule')
- Purple sage (*Salvia officinalis* 'Purpurascens')
- Common oregano (*Origanum vulgare*)
- French parsley (*Petroselinum crispum* French)
- Creeping thyme (*Thymus* 'Doone Valley')
- Fine bark chips
- Gravel or slate chips (optional)

Whether you're a serious foodie who uses only fresh ingredients in the kitchen or you're just starting out with your first herbs, there are five key plants you shouldn't be without: rosemary, sage, oregano, parsley and thyme.

For these herbs to thrive, you should give each plant its own pot. Use large pots for rosemary and oregano and medium for sage, as these all need room to grow. Add crocks to the bottom of the pots to improve drainage, before adding the compost. Oregano, sage, rosemary and thyme need a loam-based potting compost, such as John Innes No. 2, while parsley prefers a multi-purpose compost, top-dressed with fine bark chips to prevent it from drying out.

All these herbs are sun-lovers, apart from the parsley, which needs partial shade. And all will be happy in their pots for many years, except the parsley again, which is short-lived and best sown every year for a continuous supply.

TIP
Gravel or slate chips scattered over the surface of the compost not only looks tidy but will cut down moisture loss on hot summer days.

Get a taste for winter chicory

When to do it: sow in June–July, force in Nov–Dec

You will need:
- Witloof chicory seeds
- Large pots
- Old box or bin

If you long for freshly picked leaves in your food in winter, perk up your dishes with some home-grown forced chicory, which is delicious when braised or sliced up in a salad.

Witloof chicory is the best type for forcing. Sow the seeds in June or July in rows 30cm (12in) apart, then leave them to grow. In around November, dig up the chicory plants, cut off the top growth, leaving 2.5cm (1in) of leaves, and trim the roots to 20cm (8in). Store the roots in dry compost in a cool shed or garage, where they will stay dormant until you need them.

Take three or four roots at a time, to stagger your crop, and plant them in pots of compost or garden soil. Bring them inside, cover them with a box, an upturned bin or anything else that will block out the light, just as you would with rhubarb, and place them in a warm, dark location. Water occasionally, and after a few weeks new buds should appear. Wait until these are 7.5–10cm (3-4in) tall (after three to four weeks), then cut them off at the base, eat and enjoy!

TIP
Don't throw out the roots once you've harvested the leaves – each root should produce a few more shoots before you need to replace it with a fresh root from store.

Prune for better crops

When to do it: July–August

You will need:

- Secateurs

One of the joys of growing trained fruit trees is surely the ease with which you can prune them. Pruning is one of those jobs that gardeners tend to put off until they absolutely have to do it – whether it's because they don't know what to do, or because it means clambering up trees or ladders. Apple trees trained against a wall or fence as a cordon, espalier or fan do away with much of that bother.

To improve flowering performance and produce a good crop, apple trees should be pruned in early summer. This means cutting back all sideshoots growing from the main branch network to about three leaves from the cluster of leaves at their base. Any shoots growing from these need cutting back harder to just one leaf from their base.

This encourages fruiting spurs to form, which are clusters of short, thickened shoots carrying the flowers that will form your apples.

TIP

Some varieties, particularly early fruiting ones, bear their fruit on the tips of their branches. These should be pruned only in winter, removing the dead or damaged wood, because summer-pruning would cut away fruiting wood.

Boost your tomato crop When to do it: July–September

You will need:
- Tomato plants
- Bamboo canes
- Garden twine
- Watering can
- Tomato food

As summer goes on and your tomatoes are thriving and flowering, make a few regular and timely tweaks to keep your plants on track for a bumper harvest.

When plants start to bear fruit stake them before they collapse under the weight of their crop. Drive a bamboo cane into the soil next to the plant, taking care not to damage its roots, then tie the stems to the cane with twine in one or more places, depending on how much support is needed.

Mid-summer is the time to capitalise on the sunshine in order to ripen the fruit. Removing the vigorous sideshoots that develop between the side branches and the main stem is an important job, as you don't want the plant using up its energy on these leafy shoots – you want it to put all its efforts into producing tomatoes. The leafy shoots can also shade the developing fruit, hindering the ripening process. To remove a young shoot, simply grasp it at the base, close to the main stem, and bend it sharply downwards to give a clean break.

As temperatures rise, water your tomato plants on a daily basis if possible, and to keep them cropping give the plants regular doses of specialist tomato feed once you see the first tiny fruit.

TIP
If you've left a bit behind when pinching out a sideshoot, don't leave it as it may die back and damage the main stem. Pinch out the stump, taking care not to harm the adjacent growth.

Growing full flavours for autumn

When to do it: October

You will need:
- Large container
- Crocks or stones
- Loam-based potting compost
- Fine composted bark
- Garlic chives (*Allium tuberosum*)
- Parsley (*Petroselinum crispum*)
- 'Bull's Blood' beetroot (*Beta vulgaris* 'Bull's Blood')

The end of summer doesn't have to mean the end of fresh herbs plucked from the garden – some are at their most tasty at this time. Plant garlic chives, parsley and 'Bull's Blood' beetroot in a colourful container that you can move to follow the last rays of autumn sun and you can be cropping until the first frosts strike.

Place a layer of crocks in the bottom of the container to improve drainage, then half-fill it with compost, mixing three parts John Innes No. 2 to one part composted fine bark. Add the plants and top up with compost until it's a couple of centimetres below the pot's rim, to allow room for watering. As it's a mixed container, place it in partial shade, but be prepared to move it to a sunnier spot as the days get shorter.

Pick the leaves as and when you need them. When the herbs come to an end in early winter, pull up the remaining beetroots and cook the roots as a tasty vegetable.

TIP
Choose a lightweight container so that it can be easily moved, even when filled with compost and plants.

Get early rhubarb

When to do it: November onwards

You will need:

- Rhubarb plant
- Mulch
- Bucket filled with garden compost
- Black polythene, bin or forcing pot

Delicious rhubarb brings a warm glow to a dinner table, and if you force it, you can have an early crop and be eating it on cold, wintery days in February and March. Rhubarb is best grown from crowns, rather than seeds, and should be planted out in autumn. Mulch heavily after planting and water in dry weather.

You can start forcing plants in around January or February by digging up a dormant portion and planting it in a large bucket filled with garden compost. Block out any light to the stems by covering the plants with black polythene, an upturned bin or a traditional forcing pot, then place it in a dark, sheltered spot. Water the plant regularly and within about four weeks you should have mouth-wateringly tender, pink stems of rhubarb.

The unforced plants in the garden will be ready for harvesting from around late April and early May.

TIP
Forcing exhausts the rhubarb plant, so it's best to throw it away once it has finished cropping.

Grow gutsy garlic

You will need:

■ Garlic bulbs (*Allium sativum*)
■ Cloches
■ Modular seed trays (optional)
■ Multi-purpose compost and trowel (optional)

It's worth growing your own garlic for a ready supply that's fresher and tastier than anything you can buy. Plant prepared cloves in late autumn to ensure the best harvest the following summer. You can still plant in the ground through to early spring, as long as the bulbs get at least six weeks of cold in the ground.

While you can plant the shop-bought garlic that's sold for eating, the varieties aren't usually suited to the British climate so they tend to be less successful than the bulbs sold by seed suppliers. When planting, break the bulb into individual cloves, taking care not to damage them as this leads to rotting. In mild parts of Britain, plant the cloves directly outdoors into well-prepared soil, spacing them 10cm (4in) apart.

Push them into the soil so that the tip of each clove is just below the surface. Cover with cloches in frosty weather.

In cold areas, or if you have very heavy soil, plant the cloves in divided seed trays filled with multi-purpose compost. Water them well and place the trays in a cool greenhouse or cold frame to grow on. Plant them out in March or April, setting the plants at the same level at which they were growing in the trays.

TIPS

Always keep the plants well watered – if they dry out for long periods, the cloves won't swell and the resulting crop will have a short storage life. If you like the garlic you've grown, set aside a bulb to replant next autumn.

Growing fruit in small spaces

When to do it: November–March

You will need:

- Wire
- Hammer and nails
- Fruit tree
- Spade
- Granular fertiliser
- Garden compost
- Mulch

If you love the idea of fruit trees in your garden, but think you don't have enough space, think again. Trained forms of fruit trees are the perfect solution in this situation. All you need is a bare fence panel or two, and you can cover them with fan or espalier fruit trees. You can buy ready-trained fruit trees, or you can order untrained bare-root plants in winter, which are significantly cheaper.

Before planting your tree, fix horizontal wires to the fence panels, to which you can tie the branches as you train them into shape. You can attach the wires to the fence using nails, but allow a few centimetres between the fence and the wire so there's room for the stems to grow and air to circulate, which will help prevent diseases.

Dig a hole one-third wider than the tree's roots and plant the tree 15–22cm (6-9in) away from the fence, angling the trunk towards the fence. Add a handful of granular fertiliser to the soil and backfill the hole with a mix of soil and garden compost. Tie the trained branches to the wires, water well and top-dress with a layer of mulch. Water the tree regularly while it gets established.

TIP

Many apples, pears and plums need another variety nearby to ensure pollination, but some are self-fertile so you can get away with planting just one tree. Check your tree's needs before buying.

Up on the roof

When to do it: all year round

You will need:
- Bird table with a roof
- Tape measure
- Plastic sheeting, such as an old compost bag
- Water-retention matting
- Scissors
- Hammer and galvanised tacks
- Saw
- 1m (3½ft) of 50 x 12mm (2 x ½in) timber batten
- Drill, screws and screwdriver
- Craft knife
- 50 x 50cm (20 x 20in) square of sedum matting
- Slow-release fertiliser

You might want your bird table where you can see it easily and watch the visiting wildlife come and go, but when it's new and unweathered it can be a distracting focal point. Giving it a new green roof should help it blend into its natural surroundings, and it's quick and easy to put in place.

Measure the roof, cut a piece of plastic sheeting to fit, and secure it to the roof with tacks, creating a waterproof layer. Cut the water-retention matting to size and cut another piece wide enough to cover the ridge of the roof (where plants will dry out most because water will drain off quickly there). Fix the matting to the roof using tacks.

Saw the timber batten into four – two pieces for each slope of the roof. Cut one end of each piece at a 45-degree angle, then position two of the battens at each end of the roof, so they fit together neatly at the ridge. Drill some pilot holes, then screw the battens in place.

Use a craft knife to cut the sedum matting to size, then lay it over the roof. Sprinkle with slow-release fertiliser and water it well. You can buy sedum matting over the internet, or garden centres may be able to order it for you.

TIP

Don't stop at bird tables – why not use sedum matting to hide an ugly shed or garage roof, or to insulate a porch, kennel or hutch?

Welcome wildlife

You will need:

- Bricks
- 2 wooden pallets
- Thin twiggy branches
- Straw
- Cane bundles
- Roofing felt
- Hammer and tacks
- Logs
- Ridge roof tiles
- Pine cones

If you want to encourage wildlife into your garden, but don't want your space to look tatty and unkempt, why not try this stylish wildlife stack? It's smart enough for any garden and will provide an array of creatures with food and shelter. And many of these visitors will return the favour by acting as useful pollinators and predators of garden pests.

Choose a level site in sun or light shade. Arrange a layer of bricks on the ground to provide crevices for toads and other amphibians, then place a wooden pallet on top. Stuff half of the pallet with straw to provide nesting places for ladybirds and suchlike and the other half with thin, twiggy branches that will give shelter to larger insects, including butterflies. Place the second pallet on top and fill with an array of similar materials.

Tack a sheet of roofing felt or heavy-duty UV-stabilised polythene to the top of the second pallet to keep the stack dry. Make up the top layer with whatever appeals to you. We used old ridge tiles, cane bundles, pine cones and logs drilled with holes (see page 118) to provide extra habitats for insects such as bees and spiders.

TIP
If you want to blend the stack into your garden, you could cover it with a green roof of sedums (see page 90).

Top table

You will need:

- Scaffolding plank, 4m long
- Tape measure
- Pencil
- Saw
- 2 x 1m (3ft) lengths of 2 x 12cm (¾ x 4¾in) timber
- Drill
- 10 x 5cm (2in) screws
- Screwdriver
- Sandpaper
- 1 litre tin of woodstain
- Paintbrush
- 4 'Vika Inge' legs from Ikea (or similar)

Hardwearing garden furniture needn't cost the earth – even the most amateur DIY-er can put together this sturdy and stylish table at minimum expense. Spend an afternoon with your tools and you could be sitting at a top table for many summers to come.

Decide how large you want your table to be, measure and mark your plank, then cut it to size. Lay the cut planks side by side, then sit the two lengths of timber across them, one at each end, and screw them in place. Sand or plane any rough edges, and paint the table top the colour of your choice.

When the paint is dry, attach the legs according to the instructions, then pull up a chair and settle down with a coffee and newspaper.

TIP
To cut the cost, pick up old planks from a reclamation yard or call a local scaffolding company to see if they sell off old boards.

Bamboo barrier

When to do it: all year round

You will need:

- Bamboo fixing posts, 6cm x 1.3m (2½ x 4½ft)
- Saw
- Pea gravel

Stop plants straying from borders with style – spend an afternoon with a saw and some stout bamboo posts and you could liven up your lawn edges with this unique and rustic bamboo barrier.

Dig a trench about 8cm (3½in) deep along your border edge and a little wider than the diameter of the bamboo posts. Cut the bamboo into 20cm (8in) lengths – you should get six pieces from each pole. Position the cut pieces of bamboo tightly side by side in the trench, then backfill with soil to hold them in place and keep them upright. When the edging is in place, complete the look by simply filling in the hollow centres of the bamboo with pea gravel.

TIP
This edging looks great with all planting, but particularly complements bamboos and grasses.

Rack up your successes

You will need:
- Duckboard
- Drill, screwdriver and screws, or hammer and nails
- Woodstain
- Paintbrush
- Wire
- 10 hanging kitchen hooks
- Small terracotta pots
- Small plants

Here's a novel use for an ordinary bathroom duckboard – painted and hung up, it's quickly transformed into a pretty and practical rack that's perfect for neatly storing essential gardening paraphernalia and displaying your favourite plants.

Take your duckboard and apply two coats of woodstain to it, in any colour you wish. When the paint is dry, attach the board to a wall. Drill or screw through the board into the wall, or tie a loop of wire to it and hang it on a nail knocked into the wall.

Attach wire loops to your pots so you can hang them from hooks on the board. If they have a rim, tie string underneath it and knot a loop, or if they don't, pass string through the drainage holes in the base of the pots and tie the two ends into a knot at the rim. Plant up a few pots and hang them from the hooks using the string loops, and leave a few pots empty for storing secateurs, string or other odds and ends.

TIP
Add a couple of extra hooks to the board, without pots, so you can hang a watering can and other items from them.

Pebble mosaic table

You will need:
- Cheap metal table
- 30mm (1¼in) pebbles (enough to cover the table top)
- Clear exterior varnish and paint brush
- Glue gun and glue sticks

Give your garden the personal touch by customising a cheap bistro table with a pretty pebble mosaic. Just one afternoon's work will give you a practical and attractive new garden feature, without breaking the bank.

Before you begin, make sure the surface of the table is clean, and wash any pebbles that have traces of grit. Once clean and dry, arrange the pebbles on the table top in your chosen pattern. Make sure the pebbles sit at about the same height, so the top is roughly level.

Glue a small area of pebbles at a time, adjusting any irregularities in their heights by building up the level with more glue. Continue until all the pebbles are glued, then leave them to dry thoroughly. Once you're satisfied that the pebbles have dried completely, coat the table top with a few layers of varnish for extra durability.

TIP
Bring the table into a conservatory or shed over winter to protect it from frost, and to help prolong the life of your mosaic.

Put yourself at the cutting edge

When to do it: all year round

You will need:
- Building sand
- Cement
- Bricks or paviours
- Spade
- Spirit level
- Rubber mallet

If the edges of your lawn are looking a little the worse for wear, a mowing strip could be the answer. Whether you use bricks or paviours, this attractive design feature can prevent damage to the edge of your lawn and make your grass look neater without the need for arduous trimming.

The bricks need to be set so that their tops are level with the soil surface, allowing the lawnmower to glide over the grass and the bricks. To create this level edge, dig a small trench along the edge of the lawn to the depth of one brick plus an extra 5–8cm (2-3in) to allow for the mortar base.

Mix the mortar using five parts building sand to one part cement, making a small batch each time so it doesn't set before you're ready to use it. Spread a 5–8cm (2-3in) layer in the base of your trench, along a short section, then place the bricks carefully in a single row on top. Tap each brick into the mortar using a rubber mallet and check the top is level with the surface of the lawn as you go along. Mix the next batch of mortar as you need it, then add the next section of bricks, and repeat until the edging is complete. Leave it over night to set, before backfilling on either side of the row with topsoil or gravel.

TIP
Edging like this is great for preventing gravel straying from paths on to lawns. It can also stop ground-covering plants and bark mulch spilling on to the grass.

Rack 'em up
When to do it: all year round

You will need:
- A length of 70 x 15mm (2¾ x ⅝in) planed timber
- Paint
- Electric drill 3.5mm timber drill bit
- Bradawl (screwdriver-like tool for making holes)
- 32 and 25mm (1¼ and 1in) tool clips
- Screwdriver
- Screws

When the garden lies dormant over winter, make the most of this quiet time to prepare for the busy season ahead and get your shed ship-shape. Garden jobs are much easier when you know where everything is, and this useful rack is just the thing to keep your tools organised. It'll only take an hour to make and you don't need to be a whizz at DIY to put it together.

Take a length of timber and cut it to fit the space where you intend to put it. Give the wood a coat of paint and leave it to dry. Drill a hole through each end of the timber, about 2cm (1in) in from the edge. Using a bradawl, make holes where you want the tool clips to go, spacing them 10cm (4in) apart along the centre of the timber. Screw the tool clips to the timber through the holes made with the bradawl, then screw the rack to your shed wall using the holes you made at each end. Once it's in place, hang up your tools and enjoy your tidy shed.

TIP
Keep your work bench tidy by making a rack for hanging up your hand tools too.

Wise ways with water

When to do it: all year round

You will need:
- Old hosepipe
- Bradawl (screwdriver-like tool for making holes)
- Spade

If your old hosepipe has seen better days and is springing leaks all along its length, don't throw it out, use it to gradually seep water to your plants instead. A seep hose is environmentally friendly because it delivers the water right to where it's needed, so less is wasted through run-off or evaporation. It has the added bonus, too, of saving you money if your water is metered.

Take an old hosepipe and pierce holes along its length using a bradawl, then attach it to a tap at one end and a hose end-stopper at the other. If there's a distance between the tap and your border of thirsty plants, don't pierce that section, otherwise you'll be wasting water. Snake the hose around the base of your plants, burying it slightly beneath the soil surface to make it less conspicuous and get it closer to where it's needed most.

When you want to water, simply turn the tap on very low, so the water seeps rather than spurts out of the holes.

TIP
Try connecting the seep hose to your water butt – you can buy connectors for this from specialist suppliers or garden centres.

Reel it in

You will need:

- Metal or enamel bucket
- Drill or hammer and large nail
- Wing nuts
- Hose

If you're constantly tripping over your tangled mess of a hose and you've got attachments scattered all around the garden or shed, this quirky two-in-one storage system could be the ideal solution to avoid damage to both yourself and your hose. Simply punch a couple of holes in the bottom of a metal or enamel bucket using a drill, or a hammer and large nail, and attach it to a fence or shed with wing nuts.

Wrap your hose around the outside of the bucket to keep it tidy and to iron out any lumps, bumps and squashed bits. Use the space inside the bucket to store spray guns and other attachments so you can always have them to hand when you need them.

TIP
To save the effort of lugging the hose across the garden, position the bucket close to an outdoor tap.

Where the river runs dry

When to do it: all year round

You will need:

■ Weed-suppressing membrane
■ Bags of 10mm (⅜in) gravel to cover the area to a depth of 10mm (⅜)in
■ 30mm (1⅛in) pebbles and larger cobbles
■ Scissors
■ Trowel
■ Thyme
■ Grasses

In these days of hosepipe bans and water shortages, a dry garden can be a practical and attractive element in a garden design. This cobbled path evokes a dry riverbed and looks spectacular planted up with grasses and fragrant thymes.

First decide where you want your riverbed to run, and cover the ground with weed-suppressing membrane. Lay a bed of gravel 10mm (⅜in)-deep on top of this, covering the edges of the material. Using pebbles or larger cobbles, mark the outline of the riverbed, shaping its course. When you're happy with the layout, fill in the course with more pebbles, placing the larger ones at the beginning and the smallest at the end.

Cut holes in the membrane to make planting pockets and drop in thyme and grasses to soften the stone landscaping. Water the plants in, then sit back and enjoy.

TIP
To give the impression of the riverbed running beyond the horizon, make it wider at the beginning than at the end.

Cooking over coals

You will need:

- Large clay pot
- Bricks
- Kitchen foil
- Pebbles
- Charcoal
- Oven shelf or grill rack

If you don't have space for a barbecue or don't like the look of a permanent barbecue stand, why not try this clever clay-pot barbecue instead? It costs almost nothing and takes less time to make than pre-heating the oven!

Choose a large clay pot, around 40cm (16in) in diameter, and prop it up on a couple of bricks so that air can circulate, which will keep the charcoal burning while you cook. Line the inside of the whole pot with several layers of kitchen foil, folding it over the rim and pressing it tight over the outside edge.

Fill the bottom half of the pot with pebbles and top it up with charcoal. Place a shelf from the oven or a grill rack across the top of the pot and bring out the burgers.

TIP
Make your food tastier by laying aromatic prunings from lavender, rosemary or thyme on the glowing charcoal.

Whip borders into shape

When to do it: all year round, but winter is best

You will need:

- Living willow whips
- Secateurs
- String

If the dividing line between lawn and border is becoming blurred and your plants are making a bid for freedom, it's time to hold them back. This border edging is an attractive, practical way of providing support for billowing, flopping plants, and the living willow whips blend in with the plants to make a subtle, natural barrier.

Living willow is best bought in winter from specialist willow nurseries or suppliers. Before you plant it, cut about 30cm (12in) off each end of the whips. Take two whips, tie them together at one end (butt to tip), wind them around each other, then tie them securely at the other end.

To make an arch, push each end of the tied whips 15cm (6in) into prepared soil, overlapping the arches as you go. Five arches will cover about 1.8m (6ft), depending on how much they overlap.

TIP

As the willow is living, bear in mind it will sprout into leaf in spring, so you'll need to weave in or trim off new growth to keep the edging looking neat and tidy.

Pebble mulch   When to do it: January–April

You will need:
- Large pebbles

In warm weather, the soil in your beds and border can quickly become dry or be swamped with weeds. So if you'd rather spend your summer enjoying your garden rather than battling to keep problems at bay, get mulching – it'll help hold moisture in the soil and form a barrier against weeds.

Large pebbles are ideal for this dual purpose being placed over small areas of soil or on the surface of compost in pots. The joy of using this type of mulch is that it's easy on the eye and won't need replacing as often as organic materials, such as bark chippings, which rot down. If you prefer, slate chippings, gravel or other decorative stone chippings will work just as well.

Before you lay your pebble mulch, make sure the area is clear of weeds and the soil is moist. Water the ground if necessary as it's harder to wet soil once the mulch is in place. Scatter the pebbles, leaving a gap just around the stems of plants. Don't pack the pebbles down too tightly as you want water to filter through the gaps and get to the soil.

TIP
The best time to mulch is in late winter or early spring, when many weeds are dormant and the ground is naturally wet, so it's easier to trap moisture.

Make room for bees

You will need:

- 30cm (12in) log of fine-grained, untreated wood
- Electric drill
- Drill bits ranging in size from 3–8mm

As winter turns to spring, it's not just gardeners who are eager to get out into the garden – female mason bees are also champing at the bit to look for a space to lay their eggs. The female mason bee is not an aggressive insect, and is a great help to gardeners as she pollinates flowers and fruit blossom around the garden. Since much of her life is spent searching for hollow stems in which to lay her eggs, why not make life easier for her by turning an old log into a cosy bee hotel?

Simply drill lots of holes of different sizes into both ends of the log, as deep as the drill bits will reach. Position the finished log in a sunny spot, perhaps in an existing log pile, making sure it's sheltered from the rain. Once you've set the log in position, leave it alone – the bees will find it in the spring and hopefully enjoy their five-star accommodation.

TIP
Don't try to make quirky, wiggly holes in logs for a more natural look – a drill is ideal because the holes need to be straight for the female to lay her eggs in them.

A pond in a pot

When to do it: spring or summer

You will need:

- Frost-proof glazed bowl, 60cm (2⅜in) in diameter
- Pond waterproofing paint
- All-purpose silicone sealant or epoxy putty
- 2 round aquatic planting baskets
- Aquatic compost or heavy loam
- Dwarf waterlily, such as *Nymphaea* 'Pygmaea Helvola'
- *Acorus gramineus* 'Variegatus'
- Washed pea gravel
- 2 bricks

Make a sunny spot sparkle with this perfectly proportioned pond in a pot. Add a few dainty aquatic plants and it'll brighten up a dull corner.

Choose a bowl-shaped container with a large surface area for maximum effect – glass-fibre or plastic ones will save you time as you won't need to waterproof them. If you prefer to use a ceramic or terracotta pot, make sure it is frost proof and seal it with waterproofing paint. Fill any drainage holes with silicone sealant or epoxy putty.

Position the container where you want it to go before planting. Half-fill a planting basket with compost or heavy loam and firm it down. Spread out the roots of the waterlily on top, then fill in with more compost or loam, firming it in layers. Weight it down with plenty of pea gravel. Plant the acorus in the same way in the second basket.

Place the bricks in the bottom of the bowl, then fill it with water. Slowly lower the baskets on to the bricks. Surround the pond with other pots for an eye-catching display.

TIP

Use rainwater to fill the pond if possible, as the mains supply contains nutrients that can encourage algae and turn the pond water green in warmer weather.

Holiday watering system

You will need:
- Large bucket
- Water
- Pot or bricks
- Long strips of cotton, towelling or capillary matting

If you're worried about going away this summer because you've got no one reliable to water your plants, try this ingenious self-watering system. Fill a bucket with water and place it on top of an upturned pot or a stack of bricks. Arrange all the pots you want watered around the base of the bucket, and water them very well.

Make sure your strips of fabric are long enough to reach from the bottom of the bucket of water all the way down into the pots below. Soak your strips of fabric in water until they are thoroughly wet: these are your 'wicks'. Tuck one end of each wick into the compost of each pot, burying it slightly below the surface, and place the other end in the bucket of water.

The water will soak down the wick and into the pots, keeping the compost moist for as long as the bucket has water in it. If you want to water lots of plants, set up a few such watering systems so the water isn't used up too quickly.

TIP
To keep the system going as long as possible, you need to slow down the rate at which the bucket empties. In hot, dry weather, place the bucket in the shade to reduce loss of water by evaporation.

Clever cloche

You will need:
- Hanging baskets, 35cm (14in) in diameter
- Pack of glazng film
- Double-sided tape
- Scissors
- Hairdryer

Keep autumn sowings snug through the winter or warm up the soil for spring seedlings with these clever home-made cloches. Made from hanging baskets and secondary glazing film, they echo traditional Victorian bell cloches but cost a fraction of the price.

Each cloche will take minutes to make and will last for a good few months in the winter wet. If they do break or get damaged, simply remove and replace the film.

To make each cloche, cover the hanging basket with a piece of glazing film, attaching it at the rim with double-sided tape. Leave about 5cm (2in) of film overhanging the edge. Use a hairdryer to blow the film until all the wrinkles disappear and it tightens. Snip off the surplus film with a pair of scissors.

TIP
To secure the cloche without puncturing it, mould a length of garden wire around the cloche and anchor it to the ground using pegs.

Meadow in a pot

When to do it: March–April

You will need:

- Shallow terracotta bowl
- Crocks
- Multi-purpose compost
- 5 cowslip plants (*Primula veris*)
- Small pieces of turf

If you dream of seeing a wildflower meadow from your window, but only have a small patio garden or balcony, why not make your own spring meadow in a bowl? Buy potted cowslips in March or April, and all you need to do is plant them up to create a bright display.

Put a layer of crocks in the bottom of a shallow bowl and then half-fill it with compost. Knock the plants out of their pots and arrange them in the bowl. Once you're happy with the spacing, top up the bowl with compost, firming it around the plants with your fingers. Cover any visible bare soil with patches of turf to give the pot a meadow feel.

TIP
Leave the plants in the bowl once they've finished flowering – the cowslips and turf will quickly knit together to create a natural look that will become more authentic every year.

Salvage style

When to do it: March–April

You will need:

- Various salvaged containers
- Car paint (optional)
- Multi-purpose compost
- Horticultural grit
- Gravel and decorative pebbles
- Herbs
- Alpine plants
- Brightly coloured pelargonium
- 2 bedding plants

You don't need expensive pots to create a stylish effect on your patio. With a little imagination you can turn any discarded odds and ends that are lurking in corners around the garden into fun, colourful containers.

In this varied arrangement for a sunny spot, we planted a selection of alpine plants in an old sink filled with compost and grit, and crammed a metal bucket full of handy culinary herbs. The bright red containers were once industrial-sized drainage pipes, but when sprayed with car paint and planted up with seasonal bedding they became cheerful containers to liven up a drab patio. To finish off our pots, we added pebbles as a decorative mulch.

Finally, to add height to the arrangement, we planted a single vibrant pelargonium into an old chimney stack instead of the more traditional terracotta pot.

TIP
If you don't have anything to hand that you can transform into a stylish container, take a trip to a reclamation yard or have a rummage in a junk shop or jumble sale – you could pick up some real bargains.

Chill-out zone

When to do it: May

You will need:

- Large terracotta pot
- Small terracotta pot
- Cream emulsion and paintbrush
- Crocks
- Multi-purpose compost
- Slow-release fertiliser
- Water-retaining granules
- Mother-in-law's tongue (*Sansevieria trifasciata* var. *laurentii*)
- Ivy (*Hedera helix* 'Anita)
- 3 pineapple lilies (*Eucomis bicolor*)
- 3 asparagus ferns (*Asparagus densiflorus*)

Seek respite from the hot summer sun by retreating into a shady corner to relax with this calming combination of plants. Cool, cream pots are kinder on the eyes than white on a bright day, and the subtle colours and contrasting shapes and textures of the plants have a restful air.

Give the pots two coats of emulsion each for good colour and coverage, then, when dry, position them in shade or part-shade. Place plenty of crocks in the bottom of each pot, and half-fill with multi-purpose compost mixed with slow-release fertiliser and water-retaining granules.

Divide the plants between the two pots. Plant the mother-in-law's tongue at the back of the smaller pot, with the ivy in front, and plant the pineapple lilies near the front of the larger pot, with the asparagus fern frothing behind it. Fill the pots with more compost and firm it down around the plants' roots. Water in well.

TIP
Move the mother-in-law's tongue and asparagus ferns to a frost-free place over winter. The ivy and pineapple lilies are more hardy and will be fine outside.

Leafy glade

When to do it: May

You will need:

■ Old metal bucket
■ Drill
■ Crocks
■ Loam-based compost
■ Water-retaining gel
■ Slow-release fertiliser
■ 2 Japanese painted ferns (*Athyrium niponicum* var. *pictum*)
■ *Begonia* 'Escargot'
■ 2 *Pelargonium* 'Deerwood Lavender Lass'

Give a shady corner a lift in summer with this simple combination of striking plants. Although they're not obvious companions, begonias, pelargoniums and ferns all enjoy a lightly shaded spot and complement one another beautifully – the begonia and ferns provide shape and texture, while the delicate pelargonium flowers add a dash of colour.

The display is quick and easy to make. Simply drill some holes in the bottom of the bucket and add a layer of crocks to aid drainage. Half-fill the bucket with compost mixed with water-retaining gel and slow-release fertiliser.

Knock the plants out of their pots and arrange them in the bucket. This display is designed to be seen from one direction, so we placed the begonia at the front, with the ferns and pelargoniums behind it. To finish off, add a little more compost and firm it down around the plants' roots. Then water in well.

Before the first frosts, remove the begonia and pelargoniums, pot them up and take indoors. The ferns can be planted in the garden.

TIP
Keep the display looking fresh by deadheading the pelargoniums regularly to encourage more flowers.

Summer sirens

When to do it: May

You will need:

- Large pot
- Crocks
- Peat-free, multi-purpose compost
- Water-retaining gel
- Slow-release fertiliser
- 2 *Carex comans*
- 3 *Osteospermum* 'Orange Symphony'
- 3 *Heuchera* 'Purple Petticoats'

If you have a space in your garden or on your patio that needs a splash of summer colour, this is the ideal container display. It doesn't need advance planning or sowing, so it's great for an instant boost.

Place a layer of crocks in the bottom of the pot to aid drainage, then half-fill with compost mixed with water-retaining gel and slow-release fertiliser. Position the plants in the pot with the two carex in the centre, and the heucheras and osteospermums alternating around it.

Put the container in a sunny spot and remember to water it regularly – it should stay colourful and eye-catching until the first frost.

TIP
When the osteospermums have finished flowering, replace them with autumn bedding, such as nerines or cyclamens, to keep the display going.

Go for the glow

When to do it: May

You will need:

- 35cm (14in) metalware hanging basket
- Grass clippings
- Old compost bag
- Multi-purpose compost or peat-free alternative
- Water-retaining gel
- Morning Glory (*Ipomoea* 'Sweet Caroline')
- *Osteospermum* 'Nairobi Purple'
- 3 *Calibrachoa* 'Million Bells Cherry'
- 6 *Diascia* 'Red Ace'
- Slow-release fertiliser pellets or high-potash feed

This summer, go for a truly eye-catching display with this large hanging basket packed with contrasting colours and trailing, vibrant flowers. To plant it up, sit the basket in a bucket and line it with thick clumps of moist grass clippings. Add a layer of plastic inside this to help retain moisture and to hold the grass in place. An old compost bag is ideal for this – just cut it to fit and lay the black side facing outwards. Snip drainage holes into the plastic, then fill the basket two-thirds full with compost mixed with water-retaining gel.

Take the morning glory and osteospermum out of their pots, tease out the roots and plant them off-centre. Then add the calibrachoas and diascias around the edge, where their flowers will soon trail over the side of the basket. Push in some slow-release plant food – around five pellets per 35cm (14in) basket – or water once a week with a high-potash feed. Give the plants a thorough watering before hanging the basket up, and remember to water at least once a day in hot weather.

TIP

When planting up a large basket, place an 8cm (3in) pot in the centre with its rim just above the compost. Then always water directly into the pot, so the moisture goes straight to the plant roots.

If it's broke, don't fix it   When to do it: May–June

You will need:
- Broken flower pot
- Multi-purpose compost
- Horticultural grit
- Tray of Livingstone daisies (*Mesembryanthem-ums*)

Don't throw away broken pots or smash them up for use as crocks – turn them into special features by adding some vibrant daisies.

Lay the broken pot on its side and fill it with compost mixed with horticultural grit in equal measures. Take a tray of plug-grown Livingstone daisies and push the roots of each one deep into the compost. Cover any exposed roots with more compost, then firm down and water in well.

For a tidy finish and to keep the foliage away from damp soil, sprinkle a layer of grit over the surface of the compost. The plants will quickly be covered with vibrant daisy flowers that burst open in the warmth of the summer sun.

TIP
These plants are tender, so overwinter them in a frost-free place or simply replace them every year.

A taste of the Wild West

When to do it: May–June

You will need:
- Stainless steel container
- Drill
- Crocks or stones
- Loam-based compost
- Horticultural grit or sand
- *Euphorbia ingens*
- 10 grey-green echeverias
- Bag of polished river pebbles

Bring a flavour of the Wild West's sun-baked plains to your garden with this clean and elegant arrangement of arresting plants. Both the euphorbia and echeverias love really well-drained conditions, so if your container doesn't have drainage holes, drill plenty into the base. Add a layer of crocks, then fill the pot two-thirds full, using a 50:50 mix of loam-based compost and horticultural sand or grit.

Plant the euphorbia in the centre of the container, making sure the compost is at the same level as it was in the pot – to the top of its rootball. Space the echeverias evenly around the edge of the container and bed in with compost, firming as you go. Water the plants in well.

For an elegant finish, scatter a pebble mulch over the surface of the compost – we used black ones. Place the container where it will get plenty of sun, and raise it up on pot feet to improve the drainage. Move the display to a sheltered spot or under cover in winter.

TIP
To stop the drill slipping when making drainage holes, stick masking tape over the area where you'll be drilling.

Love me tender

When to do it: May–June

You will need:

■ Copper water tank or gunmetal-finish zinc pot

■ Drill

■ Old, small plastic pots

■ Loam-based compost

■ Water-retaining granules

■ Slow-release fertiliser

■ Glory flower (*Tibouchina urvilleana*)

■ 3 silver *Helichrysum petiolare*

■ 2 *Pelargonium* 'Harvard'

■ 3 *Begonia* 'Non-Stop Red'

■ 2 *Tradescantia pallida* 'Purpurea'

Metallic pots make an excellent foil for a wide range of foliage and flower colours. In this display, the deep violet foliage of the tradescantia combines with the rich red flowers of the pelargonium and begonia, above a bed of silver helichrysum leaves, and bursting through them all is the dramatic purple-blue glory flower.

Creating this striking arrangement is simple. First, drill holes in the bottom of your container if there are none already, then add a layer of upturned plastic pots to aid drainage. Fill the container with loam-based compost to within 10cm (4in) of the rim. Mix in a slow-release fertiliser and water-retaining granules.

Plant the glory flower first, right in the centre, then arrange all the other plants around the edge so they trail over. Fill any gaps with more compost and firm down. The surface should be 3cm (1in) below the rim to allow for watering. Then water the plants in well, and continue watering regularly all summer.

TIP
The glory flower isn't hardy, so move the display inside before the first frosts, or lift the plant, pot it up and keep it at a minimum of 5°C through the winter.

Cloud nine

When to do it: May–June

You will need:

- 35cm (14in) metal hanging basket
- Grass clippings
- Sheet of plastic
- Peat-free multi-purpose compost
- Water-retaining gel
- Slow-release fertiliser
- 5 *Nemesia* 'Blue Lagoon'
- 3 *Nemesia* 'Golden Eye'
- 3 purple-veined petunias
- 5 *Helichrysum* 'Gold'

Create a cloud on a clear summer's day with the pale gold, felty leaves of helichrysum, seen through a haze of frothy nemesia flowers. Helichrysums grow happily in sun or part-shade, so this arrangement is ideal for brightening up a dull corner.

Stand the basket in a bucket to hold it steady, then line it with thick clumps of moist grass clippings. Hold this in place with a sheet of plastic, cut to fit, which will help retain moisture in the compost. Cut drainage holes in the plastic and fill the basket two-thirds full with compost mixed with water-retaining gel and slow-release fertiliser.

Place the five Nemisia Blue Lagoon in the centre of the basket to get the best of both its upright and trailing flowers, then plant the smaller, darker 'Golden Eye' immediately in front. Position the petunias at the front of the basket, interspersed with the helichrysums. Fill between the roots with more compost, leaving the surface about 2.5cm (1in) below the basket's rim. Water in well and allow to drain before hanging the basket in position.

TIP
To prolong the display, deadhead the flowers regularly to encourage more blooms.

Sempervivum ball   When to do it: May–September

You will need:
- 2 x 35cm (14in) round-bottomed hanging baskets
- Moss for lining baskets
- Loam-based or multi-purpose compost
- Strong garden wire
- Approx 20 houseleeks (*Sempervivum*) plants (quantity depends on plant size and need for instant effect)

Looking for a low-maintenance summer basket? These plants are tolerant of dry conditions and low nutrients, and look spectacular as a hanging ball.

Take the chains off the baskets and place a good layer of moss in the bottom of one, coming up the sides by 3–5cm (1–2in). Then fill to the top of the moss with compost and firm down. Knock a sempervivum out of its pot, gently squash the rootball and ease it through a gap in the wires, so the roots sit on the surface of the compost. If you have trouble getting the rootball in, bend the wires apart to make a wider gap, but close them afterwards.

Keep adding plants until you've worked your way round the ball. Put in another layer of moss, tucking it into the neck of the plants to stop them falling out and firm compost around the roots. When the first basket is full, place the other basket upside down on top of it and tie the two together with some stout garden wire. Feed in moss through the wire and firm it against the inside of the basket, then add compost. Ease in the plants as you did before, until the basket is full. Water well.

Re-attach the wires to the lower basket, and hang it up on a strong bracket that can take the weight of the finished ball.

TIP
Feed and water the ball while the plants are establishing to ensure they quickly cover the baskets. Tease out any withered flowering rosettes to encourage new ones.

Pure and simple

When to do it: October–November or January–February

You will need:

- Zinc trough
- Drill
- Crocks or stones
- Gravel or grit
- Multi-purpose compost
- 3 small hart's tongue ferns such as *Asplenium scolopendrium* 'Angustifolia'
- 12 bulbs (or 4 plants) *Iris* 'Pauline'
- 3 bird's-foot ivy such as *Hedera helix* 'Tripod'

Beat the winter blues with a windowbox of sweet perfume and cheery colour. The dwarf irises will bloom long before other bulbs in a mild winter, bringing a welcome blast of colour and scent, so put an early spring in your step with this combination of needle-like iris, filigree ivy and crimped fern.

Drill a drainage hole in each corner of the trough and cover the base with crocks, followed by a thick layer of gravel or grit, then fill it two-thirds full with compost. Remove the ferns from their pots and tease out the roots. Position them along the length of the trough at even intervals.

Plant the bulbs in four groups, dotting them between the ferns. If you plant this up in autumn, use iris bulbs, but if you do it in spring, use pots of ready-grown irises and tease out the roots before planting. Add the ivy along the front edge of the trough. Fill any gaps with more compost, firming it around the plants with your fingers. Stand the trough on a patio or windowsill in full sun or light shade.

TIP

To keep the display going once the irises are over, replace them with pot-grown 'Tête-à-tête' daffodils, and follow these with dwarf tulips in late spring.

Winter warmer

When to do it: November

You will need:

- Large dark pot
- Crocks
- Multi-purpose compost
- 3 red-stemmed dogwoods (*Cornus*)
- 6 trailing ivies (*Hedera*)
- 6 cyclamen

Celebrate the festive season long beyond Twelfth Night with this colourful Christmas container. It's a fantastically easy arrangement to plant, and will last longer than a wilting Christmas tree, with its colours staying bright all winter long.

Any pot will do, but a dark one looks most dramatic with this planting scheme. Place a layer of crocks in the base of a large container and half-fill it with compost. Knock the dogwoods out of their pots and plant them centrally, then underplant with the cyclamen. Position the ivies around the rim so they trail over the sides.

In spring, the dogwoods and ivies can be planted out into the garden if you wish. Cut back some of the stems of the dogwoods in late winter to a few buds from the base to encourage bright new stems for next year.

TIP

If you don't want the pot for something else, you can keep this as a permanent display. Just replace the cyclamen with spring bulbs or summer bedding as the seasons change.

Tub of roses

You will need:

- Large tin bath
- Drill
- Lots of crocks or stones
- Good-quality loam-based compost
- 2 roses – *Rosa* 'Rhapsody in Blue' and 'Boule de Neige'
- 3 *Heuchera* 'Licorice'
- 2 *Salvia* x *superba* 'Merleau'
- 2 small blue violas

If you love roses but haven't got space for a rose garden, plant one in a container. This salvaged galvanised bath makes a quirky and unusual home for plants, and gives the formal English rose an informal feel.

Drill lots of evenly spaced holes in the base of the bath, then place it in a sunny or lightly shaded, sheltered spot against a fence or wall while it's still empty. Put a good layer of crocks or stones in the base to aid drainage, and fill the bath two-thirds full with compost.

Plant the roses in the centre of the bath but towards the back. We used *Rosa* 'Rhapsody in Blue' to reflect the bath's grey colouring and 'Boule de Neige' to give the arrangement white highlights and fragrance. Choose roses that are naturally compact so they don't outgrow the container. Next, evenly space the heucheras around the edge, filling in the gaps with the salvias and violas. When all the plants are in, fill around them with compost, firming it with your fingers.

TIP
Give your roses a boost with a slow-release fertiliser in March, and again in July.

Keep orchids happy

When to do it: all year round

You will need:

- Potted orchid
- Orchid fertiliser
- Larger pot
- Crocks
- Orchid compost
- Drip tray and pebbles
- Secateurs

In recent years, orchids have become an affordable luxury – their elegant, long-lasting blooms make them a perfect gift and a wonderful alternative to cut flowers in the home. The problem most people have, though, is keeping them going. Orchids aren't overly fussy plants, but they do like certain conditions if they are to thrive.

Whether you're growing orchids in your home or in the greenhouse, position them out of direct sunlight, and whenever the compost looks very dry, water them thoroughly. Every third watering, add a specialist orchid feed or use a general-purpose feed at half strength.

Orchids develop a strong, fleshy root system, and when the roots fill the pot you should move the plant into a slightly larger container. Place crocks in the bottom of the new pot and cover with specialist orchid compost. Then add the plant and backfill around the rootball with compost. Don't firm it down – leave the compost loose to allow water to run straight through. Stand the pot in a drip tray of moist pebbles to increase humidity around the plant.

After flowering, cut back the stem to the base using secateurs. Don't rush to do this as some orchids, such as phalaenopsis, often produce a sideshoot that will bear a second display of flowers.

TIP
Don't let orchid plants get too hot in summer – they stop growing above 30°C so provide adequate ventilation.

Make a table-top pond

You will need:
- Large bowl, or several small ones
- Water
- Aquatic plants – such as water lettuce (*Pistia stratiotes*) and water hyacinths (*Eichhornia crassipes*)

If you've always wanted a garden pond but limited space or young children prohibits it, why not make one indoors? This is a seriously scaled-down version, but here's where size doesn't matter. This container makes an unusual display in the house or a sophisticated centrepiece for a table, or you can line up individual bowls for a contemporary display at a dinner party.

All you need is a large container (or lots of small ones) filled with water. Float your chosen aquatic plants in the water and they'll survive in a well-lit position for as long as they fit the container. Divide them up as they start to expand, removing the outer, tattier leaves and replanting fresher, young offshoots into more bowls of water.

TIP
Water lettuce and water hyacinths are very invasive, so never dispose of them in ponds, lakes or waterways.

Pot up plug plants When to do it: May

You will need:
- Plug plants
- Pots
- Crocks
- Multi-purpose compost

Buying plug plants is an excellent way to save time and windowsill space when planting up beds, borders and even pots. There's no sowing of seeds and your work begins only when they arrive at your door.

As soon as the plants are delivered, or you get them home from the garden centre, stand them in water for a good half hour to rehydrate. The key to keeping plugs happy and healthy is to plant them up as soon as possible. If they're destined for outdoors but there's still a risk of frost, plant them into pots or large cellular trays and keep them under cover until conditions improve.

If you intend to use the plugs in pot displays, you can plant them straight into their final container. Place crocks in the bottom of each pot and half-fill with compost. Arrange the plants in the pot and backfill with compost once you're happy with the way it looks. Firm down the compost and water in the plants. With plugs destined for a border display, plant them into individual pots or trays in the same way. Place the pots in a frost-free, well-lit place until the weather improves and you can harden them off and plant them outside.

TIP
When removing plugs from their trays, always hold them by their leaves, not the stem, to prevent damage. If they're tricky to remove, push the blunt end of a pencil through the hole in the base of the tray to help ease them out.

Tackle top-heavy aeoniums

When to do it: early to mid-spring

You will need:

■ Aeonium plant
■ Secateurs
■ Seed tray or individual pots
■ Multi-purpose compost
■ Sharp sand or horticultural grit

Aeoniums are spectacular succulents that make impressive houseplants, but after a while they tend to become top-heavy and rather unstable. To keep them neat and compact, you need to cut the plants back, and as an added bonus you can use these cuttings to produce additional plants.

First you have to cut off the top of your plant, just below the point where it starts to branch. This may seem radical (not to mention distressing), but steel yourself and chop it off – the plant will be fine, and will reward you next year with lots more stems.

Once the top has gone, take off the sideshoots too and trim each to a length of 8–10cm (3-4in), Remove any straggly lower leaves from these shortened shoots and push the stems 3–5cm (1–2in) deep into individual pots, or a seed tray filled with multi-purpose compost and sharp sand or grit mixed in equal quantities. Keep the cuttings indoors in a cool, light place, out of direct sun, and water them if the compost feels dry. The cuttings should root after about two weeks, when you can transplant them into a larger pot.

TIP
Don't mist succulents or put them in a propagator where condensation could form, as they rot easily.

Install an automatic vent

You will need:
- Automatic ventilation kit
- Pencil or pen
- Screwdriver
- Screws

Do you worry about your greenhouse plants overheating on hot summer days or shivering on cold winter nights? If so, ease your fears by fitting automatic vents that will control temperatures and let your greenhouse look after itself.

Automatic vents are simple devices that respond to air temperature, opening when the air is warm and closing when it starts to cool down. The beauty of these gadgets is that they don't need electricity in order to work, and can be fitted to both aluminium and wooden frames with ease.

Ventilation kits come with complete instructions for fitting, but in general it's a straightforward job. Take the vent and place it in the centre of a window, then mark the position of the holes required for screws on both the window frame and greenhouse frame where the two meet.

Screw in the automatic vent, then check that the window can open and close. If necessary, adjust the amount the window opens by rotating the main tube of the vent opener. On a sunny day, watch and wait to see that the vent is opening properly.

TIP
It's best to fit automatic vents to windows on the side of the greenhouse that faces away from prevailing winds, to avoid strong gusts.

Take begonia leaf cuttings

When to do it: June–September

You will need:

- Healthy begonia plant
- Clean, sharp knife and cutting board
- Seed tray with cover
- Cuttings compost
- Wire or pins

You can never have too much of a good thing, and summer is the ideal time to take leaf cuttings from your favourite houseplants to increase their numbers. Just one leaf can produce many new young plants, and this technique can be used for plants such as *Begonia rex* (as here), African violets, echeverias, lilies and sedums.

Taking leaf cuttings is easy, and you don't have to disfigure your plant to do it. The key thing is to remember which way up the leaf should be kept. Remove a healthy leaf, lay it on the cutting board and, using a clean, sharp knife, cut off the excess stem. On the underside of the leaf, cut straight across each main vein, close to where the stalk was. At each of these cuts, the leaf will form a plantlet.

Place free-draining cuttings compost into a seed tray. Lay the prepared leaf the right way up on the compost and secure it with pins or bits of U-shaped wire across the veins, near the cuts. Do this with as many leaves as you wish. Water from above, put the lid on the tray, then stand it in a warm, light position.

After about four months new plantlets should have formed and will be ready for potting up individually.

TIP

If you just want to take one or two leaf cuttings, place each leaf in its own pot in exactly the same way, then cover the pot with a clear polythene bag and seal with an elastic band.

A clear choice for elegant narcissi

When to do it: September–October

You will need:

- Glass container, such as a wide jar or bowl
- Pebbles, gravel or glass beads
- Paperwhite narcissus bulbs (*Narcissus papyraceus*)

Fill your home with an early scent of spring during the dark days of winter. All you need to do is plant prepared narcissus bulbs in autumn. Narcissi are happy growing in pots of compost in the traditional way, but you could try something different and plant them in a glass container filled with gravel, glass beads or pebbles.

Take a glass jar or glass bowl that's large enough to hold the bulbs without squashing them in – bulbs look best planted in odd numbers, so aim for three or five per container. Place a layer of pebbles, gravel or glass beads in the base, then push the bulbs into the pebbles to about half their depth to hold them firm. Add water to just below the bulb and no higher, topping up to this level as and when necessary.

Put the narcissi in good light on a windowsill. White roots will quickly form, and after as little as six to eight weeks these will be followed by stems topped with fragrant flowers.

TIP
Buy enough bulbs to plant up containers every seven to ten days throughout September and early October to provide a succession of flowers in December and January.

Enjoy fragrant freesias When to do it: September–October

You will need:
- Pot
- Crocks
- Multi-purpose compost
- Freesia corms
- Split canes
- String

Few flowers are as fabulously fragrant and colourful as freesias. These native South African plants are easy to grow under cover and make beautiful blooms for cutting or displaying indoors. It's well worth planting up several pots in autumn for a really vibrant, sweet-smelling arrangement in early spring.

Prepare your pots by adding crocks and half-filling with compost. Plant the corms – around six to a 12cm (5in) pot – spacing them evenly and covering them with more compost. Place the pots in a warm, frost-free position and keep them lightly watered over winter.

Leaves will appear first, followed by the fragrant blooms. When the flower stems start to develop, begin feeding on a weekly basis with a high-potash feed. Support the stems using split canes and string or they'll topple over.

Once the display is over, continue feeding until the leaves turn yellow, then reduce the watering and let the bulbs dry off and rest until the autumn, when the cycle starts again.

TIP
Corms producing a multi-coloured display are cheap to buy, but choose heat-treated ones for more reliable results.

Plant hyacinth bulbs

When to do it: October–November

You will need:

■ Terracotta pot or bowl
■ Crocks
■ Loam-based, multi-purpose compost
■ Sharp sand
■ Hyacinth bulbs

Herald the start of spring with the spectacular blooms and knockout scent of potted hyacinths. Ready to plant in autumn, the bulbs are widely available in a broad spectrum of colours, and they look sensational when planted on their own in a rustic terracotta pot.

Spread a good layer of crocks in the bottom of your pot, half-fill it with compost mixed with a handful or two of sharp sand, and firm it down. Arrange the bulbs evenly in the pot, about 5cm (2in) apart. Cover them with a 10cm (4in)-layer of compost and water in. You can leave the pots outside until December, then bring them indoors to enjoy the flowers and fragrance.

When the flower buds appear, you may wish to repot the hyacinths into larger, decorative containers. Group together plants that are at the same stage of growth to make a series of pots that will provide a succession of flowers. Finish the pots off by putting a little moss on the surface of the compost for decoration. Keep well watered for longer-lasting flowers.

TIP
When buying bulbs to plant outdoors, avoid those that have been specially treated to flower indoors at Christmas.

Moving bananas under cover

When to do it: late autumn–early winter

You will need:
- Borderline hardy plant, such as a banana or canna
- Sharp knife
- Spade
- Fork
- Small pot to tightly fit the plant
- Multi-purpose compost

Our recent mild winters might have lulled you into a false sense of security as far as tender plants are concerned, but don't let this winter be the one when the weather catches you out. If you live in a frost-prone area or your garden isn't very sheltered, and your tender exotics are small enough to be moved, bring them indoors before the weather turns cold.

Borderline hardy plants, such as the red banana (shown here), cannas and some palms, should be dug up and put in pots under cover over winter. If you're moving a canna or a banana, first cut off the lower leaves with a knife to make the plant easier to handle. Then dig around the plant with a spade and chop back some of the rootball to make it easier to pot up. Lift the plant using a fork, and brush most of the soil from the roots. Trim off any straggly roots with a knife, so they don't rot.

Transfer the plant into a small pot containing multi-purpose compost. Water well and stand in a frost-free place over winter.

TIP
If your plant is too big to be moved, or if you don't have room under cover to store it, see page 36 for advice on wrapping plants up for winter outdoors.

Wrap up your greenhouse for winter

When to do it: late autumn–winter

You will need:

- Measuring tape
- Bubble polythene
- Scissors
- Nails, drawing pins or wire to fix the polythene in place

If your greenhouse isn't heated, it's worth insulating it with bubble polythene to keep your plants as cosy as possible through the winter. Lining all the glass with a single layer of bubble polythene will mean fewer draughts, and if you do use a heater during the very coldest days, you won't need it on as often or for so long.

Bubble polythene is readily available in garden centres, where it's sold by the metre. Choose UV-stabilised polythene that's specifically designed for greenhouses; this should last for at least three years if you look after it and store it properly. Before buying, measure the sides, roof and ends of your greenhouse so you know how much you need.

To cover the inside of your greenhouse, start with the sides, fixing the polythene to the frame using nails, drawing pins or wire, and pulling it taut for maximum insulation. When lining the roof, fix the polythene to the ridge and spread it down the glazing bars. Don't forget to cut and fasten the polythene around vents and louvres, so they can still be opened on warmer days.

TIP
Choose polythene with large bubbles as this has better insulating properties and lets in more light.

Thinking big with amaryllis

When to do it: November–February

You will need:
- Amaryllis (*Hippeastrum*) bulb (or boxed kit containing bulb, pot and compost)
- Bowl of water (to soak the bulb in)
- Large terracotta pot
- Crocks
- Bulb fibre or multi-purpose compost

Wake up dark, dismal winter days with a trumpet call of bold, bright amaryllis. These sumptuous blooms will bring colour to your windowsill in the depths of winter and make fabulous gifts over the festive season.

Huge amaryllis bulbs already have their flower bud inside, so they couldn't be simpler to grow. First you need to soak the bulb and its thick roots in a bowl of tepid water for a few hours before planting, then snip off any damaged roots. Place crocks over the drainage holes in the pot and half-fill it with bulb fibre or multi-purpose compost. Break up any lumps and lightly firm the compost with your fingers.

Set the bulb in place, spread out its roots, then trickle more compost around it until it's half-buried. Water well and put the amaryllis in a well-lit position to grow on. If you don't already have a bud, one should appear in a few weeks.

TIP
Stand your amaryllis in a cool room with plenty of light and turn the plant daily to keep growth upright. Particularly tall varieties may need supporting with split canes.

Repot succulents When to do it: late winter

You will need:
- Large terracotta pot
- Crocks or pebbles
- Free-draining compost
- Horticultural grit

If your succulent is looking a little top-heavy or seems to be trying to escape from its pot, then it's time to move it to a bigger container. New rosettes can throw a plant slightly off balance, but repotting it will give it better stability.

To repot your plant, as with this *Haworthia attenuata*, gently remove it from its current container and move it to a larger one that has pebbles or crocks in the bottom and is half-filled with free-draining compost. Fill any gaps with more compost and firm down gently, then water in.

Finally, top-dress the compost with a layer of grit – this ensures the leaves don't touch any damp compost and, quite simply, gives an attractive finish. Place the pot back in a warm spot. Your plant should be happy in its new pot for a couple of years.

TIP
Terracotta or other clay pots are ideal for succulents as they provide extra weight and stability.

Make a spiral ivy display

You will need:

- 4m (13ft) length of galvanised wire
- Wire cutters
- 1.5m (5ft) bamboo cane
- 45cm (18in) terracotta pot
- Compost
- Ivy plant (*Hedera*)

If you love a touch of topiary, but want to avoid the expense of ready-trained plants, why not have a go at making your own? All you need is a metal spiral support and an ivy plant. The ivy will soon cover the spiral to give you an elegant evergreen display at a fraction of the cost of clipped topiary. Everything you need is available from DIY stores or garden centres.

Using wire cutters, snip off a 3m (10ft) length of wire and bend it into a spiral – place it flat on the ground to do this, so it doesn't tangle and so you can see it taking shape. Wrap the central curl of the spiral around the top of the cane, leaving a little spare wire overhanging. Bend this spare wire back on itself and push it down into the top of the cane.

Fill the pot with compost, and position the cane and spiral in its centre. Cut several small pieces of wire and bend them in half to secure the spiral at the base. Plant an ivy at the foot of the spiral and train the stems up the wire, tying them gently into position with soft twine. As the plant grows, keep on tying in the new shoots and cut off any wayward stems to keep a neat spiral shape.

TIP
If you want a brighter display, or just a different effect, try using variegated ivy. You'll get that topiary look with a twist.

Herbs to hand

When to do it: all year round

You will need:

- Treated timber 1.5 x 144 x 45mm (1 x 5 x 2in)
- Ruler and pencil
- Electric drill
- 20mm wood drill bit
- 2.4m (8ft) of 2cm (1in) dowel
- Saw
- Waterproof wood glue
- Coloured wood-stain and paintbrush
- 6mm wood drill bit
- 7mm masonry drill bit
- 2 x 100mm (4in) 10-gauge screws and wall plugs
- 5 terracotta pots, 15cm (6in) in diameter
- 5 culinary herb plants

There's no excuse for flavourless food with this handy herb rack, which will add zest to your meals as well as to a dull wall. Take the length of timber and a pencil, and mark where you want the pegs. Each pair of pegs should be slightly closer together than the diameter of your pots. Leave about 10cm (4in) between each pair.

Using a 20mm wood drill bit, drill through each mark. Cut 10 lengths of dowel, each about 20cm (8in) long, and one shorter length for the watering can. Squeeze glue into the holes and push in the dowel pegs, making sure they're straight. Once the glue is dry, apply two coats of woodstain.

Using a 6mm wood drill bit, make a hole at each end of the rack. Hold the rack level on the wall and mark through the holes with a pencil. Then drill holes with a masonry drill bit and fix your herb rack in place with long screws and wall plugs. Finally, pot up your herbs and place them on the rack.

TIP
Buy extra paint so that you've got an exact match should you want to give it a new, fresh coat when the colour starts to fade.

Canny lanterns   When to do it: all year round

You will need:

- Several empty food tins
- Electric drill with a 3.5mm bit
- Car spray paint
- Galvanised wire
- Tea lights

If you think you should recycle more, here's the perfect way to turn old metal food tins into funky lanterns. They're easy to make and certainly won't break the bank. Protected from the elements with spray paint, these metal lanterns look great and will brighten up your night garden for years to come.

Wash and dry all the tins and make sure the rims are smooth. Then slowly drill evenly spaced holes through the side of each tin, carefully controlling the drill speed. Make two holes at the top of each tin, opposite one another, for the wire handle.

Take the tins outside and spray them with car paint. Use cool blue to create a calm mood. When the paint is dry, attach the handles. Make these from galvanised wire, bent around a tin to create a curved shape. Push each end through the holes and bend the ends back on themselves to make them secure.

TIP
Spray all the lanterns the same colour for a co-ordinated look, or go for many bright colours to create a party atmosphere.

Wooden spoon markers in herb pots

When to do it: all year round

You will need:

- Wooden spoons
- Craft acrylic paint
- Waterproof permanent marker

For any cook, there's nothing more practical and handy than having herbs for picking within easy reach. As well as being useful, herbs also make attractive plants in pots or in a windowbox by the kitchen, and these sunshine-yellow plant markers add a quirky and decorative reminder of what you're growing. They're also cheap and take minutes to make.

We used bright yellow paint because it looks great against the variegated thyme and lush green foliage, but you can use any colour that contrasts with your plants. Take your wooden spoons and coat them in acrylic paint. Leave them to dry, then, with the handle pointing downwards, write the name of each herb on a different spoon using the marker pen. Push the handle into the appropriate pot to label your plants.

TIP
Check the spoon handles are the right length before you paint them – you may need to cut them shorter if you're using shallow pots.

Lighten up

You will need:

- Fan trellis
- Tree stake
- Hammer and small nails
- Woodstain
- Bronze-effect planter
- Soil-based compost
- Garden fairy lights
- Fine wire
- Pliers and strong scissors
- Protective gloves
- Lavender plant

Don't let bad light stop play when you're entertaining alfresco in summer. Here's a stylish way to add sparkle to your patio using a piece of trellis, a metal planter, outdoor fairy lights and fragrant plants. The display can be left outside in all weathers and will provide magical, subtle lighting for parties or dinners in the garden on warm summer evenings. The lavender in the planter provides a relaxing scent, or you could train jasmine or honeysuckle up the trellis for heady evening scent.

To create the display, nail the trellis to the tree stake and paint both with woodstain. Fill the container with compost and push in the trellis and stake, firming it in well so it's stable. Starting with the electrical plug at the base, wrap the fairy lights around the vertical trellis timbers and secure with wire. Finally, plant lavender or fragrant climbers at the base of the trellis.

TIP

For a festive touch at Christmas, plant the container with a berrying skimmia and some ivy trailing over the edge.

Chalk it up

When to do it: all year round

You will need:
- Terracotta pots
- Blackboard paint
- Paintbrushes
- Chalk
- Compost and plants

If you move plants in and out of pots faster than you can write out new labels, here's a novel way of keeping tabs on what you've planted – labels you can write on and wipe off, and which won't go astray. All you need is a few old pots and some blackboard paint, and you can use them again and again.

Terracotta pots are ideal for this as they're chunkier than plastic and more stable for writing on, and it's a great way of reviving old pots that are marked or looking a bit tired. Paint the outside of each pot with blackboard paint – if one coat isn't enough, apply a second one once the first is dry. Then simply add compost and a plant, and write the name of the plant on the outside of the pot using chalk. It could not be simpler.

When you change the contents of the pot, wipe off the writing with a damp cloth and re-name.

TIP
If left in the rain, the chalk will come off, so these pots are best used indoors, in a greenhouse or conservatory, or in a sheltered spot.

Stars of the theatre

When to do it: all year round, but plants flower in spring

You will need:
- Small box shelf unit
- 1 litre tin darker woodstain
- 1 litre tin lighter woodstain
- Paint brushes
- Masking tape
- 2 auricula plants

Celebrate a bit of our gardening heritage with this scaled-down version of an auricula theatre, the traditional way to showcase these beautiful plants. Auriculas, with their tiny, intricately patterned flowers, are often bred for show, but any gardener can grow them to enjoy their exquisite beauty. The different flowers are all works of art in their own right and deserve a starring role on their own stage.

To make this little auricula theatre, paint the inside of the box shelf with two coats of the darker woodstain, then paint the remaining areas with two coats of the lighter colour. When dry, hang the box against a plain background using the fixings supplied with it, then add the auricula plants.

TIP
Use masking tape when painting the box to ensure a crisp line between the colours.

Hearts and flowers

When to do it: February

You will need:

- Assortment of leaves
- Piece of paper and pen
- Small pair of scissors
- Candles in glass jars
- Raffia

For a really romantic Valentine's Day meal, dine by candlelight with hearts and flowers. And add your own personal touch to the evening by decorating glass candle holders with leaves cut with a simple, heart-shaped motif.

Draw a small heart on a piece of paper and cut it out. Using this as a template, draw a heart on the back of each leaf, lining it up centrally on the vein. With a small pair of scissors, make an incision in the centre of the heart drawn on the leaf, then carefully cut outward from this to make a heart-shaped hole. Cut the edges as smoothly as possible.

Tie the leaves to the glass jars using a piece of raffia, secured with a decorative knot.

TIP
You can also tie some of the leaves around a vase to complete the table arrangement.

Home-made seed packets

When to do it: August–October

You will need:

- Brown paper cash envelopes (available from stationery shops)
- Camera or old gardening magazines
- Glue
- Marker pen

Saving seed from your favourite plants is a great way to fill out your borders for free, and autumn is the ideal time to collect seed from summer-flowering plants. But how do you keep track of what you've collected? These home-made paper seed packets are the ideal solution, offering a visual reminder, along with ideal storage conditions.

Simply take photographs of any flowers in bloom whose seeds you want to collect, then print out the pictures to a size that fits the envelopes. Glue the pictures to the front of the envelopes and label them with a marker pen. Add the seeds as you collect them, then store until it's time to start sowing.

TIP

If you don't have a camera, cut pictures of the relevant plants out of old gardening magazines or seed catalogues.

Ghoulish garlic When to do it: October

You will need:

■ 5 garlic bulbs
(*Allium sativum*)
with their stems
still attached
■ Handful of
Chinese lanterns
(*Physalis
alkekengri*)
■ Several twigs
■ Thin florist's
wire
■ Orange raffia
■ Wire cutters

If your artistic skills don't stretch to carving pumpkins, or you just fancy doing something different this Halloween, try making this simple yet stunning door decoration. With a few bulbs of garlic, some twigs and Chinese lanterns, you can give visitors a warm welcome, while keeping ghouls and vampires at bay.

Gather together five garlic bulbs, making sure they have their stems still attached, and bind them securely with a length of florist's wire. Add a number of bare twigs to the garlic to give it some volume, and use a little more wire to tie them all together. Next, add the Chinese lanterns – place them beneath the garlic bulbs, and secure the bundle with more wire.

As a finishing touch, hide the wire under a bow made from raffia, before turning the decoration the other way up and hanging it on your front door.

TIP
If you don't have physalis in your garden, buy stems from a florist or garden centre. You can even get some pretty good fake ones, too.

Halloween glow When to do it: October

You will need:

- 10 x 15cm (4 x 6in) picture frames (4 per lantern)
- Black water-resistant paint
- Small hinges and clasps (6 hinges and 1 clasp per lantern)
- Small screwdriver
- Sticky-backed plastic
- Plasti-kote etching spray
- Tea light

This year, light the way for trick-or-treaters on Halloween night with a different kind of spooky glow. Unlike the traditional carved pumpkin, these fun lanterns will last from year to year and they're also cheap, quick and easy to make.

Carefully remove the glass, discard the backing board, and paint the picture frames black. When the paint is dry, screw two hinges to one long side of each frame. Then attach one frame to the next one, using the hinges, until you have four in a row. Connect the first and last end together with a clasp to form a lantern.

Draw spooky images, such as pumpkins, bats and ghosts, on the sticky-backed plastic, then cut round the outlines and stick one on to each piece of glass removed from the frames. Apply etching spray to the glass, leave to dry and remove the plastic. Put each piece of the decorated glass into a frame and secure in place. Add a night light to the middle of the lantern.

TIP
Look out for black frames that don't need painting to make the job even quicker!

Eat your heart out

When to do it: October–March

You will need:

- 90cm (3ft) length of 2mm (⅛in)-thick galvanised wire
- Pliers
- Peanuts in shells
- String

Keep the birds in your garden happy with a peanut wreath. Hang it up in autumn and replenish throughout the winter, and you'll keep your feathered friends happy and well fed for months.

Making the wreath is easy and takes no time at all. Use pliers to cut the length of wire and bend it in half. Then bend the two loose ends up and curve them round into a heart shape. Use the pliers again to turn over 1cm (⅜in) of wire at one loose end to make a loop.

With the unlooped end of the wire, skewer through the centre of each peanut shell and slide them on until the heart is full. Thread the loose end of wire through the looped end, and bend it back on itself into a hook using pliers. Hang up the peanut heart in the garden with string. When all the peanuts have been eaten, simply unhook the wire and restock the heart with more peanuts.

TIP
If you want to leave out extra nuts for birds over winter, don't give them salted nuts – birds can't process salt, and too much of it kills them.

Natural Christmas tree

When to do it: December

You will need:
- Pot-grown birch, such as *Betula utilis* var. *jacquemontii*
- 10 litre container
- Multi-purpose compost
- Home-grown decorations
- Ribbon
- Raffia

A tree is for life, not just for Christmas. This white-stemmed birch makes an elegant alternative to the traditional Christmas conifer and can be planted out in the garden once the celebrations are over. Its fine, delicate branches are ideal for hanging decorations from, and there are no needles to keep hoovering up.

Choose a well-branched tree with a long, pale stem, and find a large, attractive container to put it in. Place the pot where you want the display, with a drip tray underneath it. Bear in mind that the tree will be happiest in a cool spot, away from heaters or fireplaces. Half-fill the pot with compost and position the tree in the centre, then top up with more compost and firm it in around the rootball. Water well, and continue to water it occasionally over the festive season until you move the tree outside.

Keep the decorations simple. We chose natural decorations and used dried oranges, pine cones and bunches of poppy seedheads. We gave them a festive touch by tying them to the tree with ribbon bows and raffia.

TIP
You can buy natural decorations, but it's also fun to make your own. To dry oranges, put them in the oven on the lowest heat possible for two hours.

Christmas decorations from nature

When to do it: December

You will need:

- Dried teasels
- Gold spray paint
- Ribbons
- Beads
- Florist's wire

It's December, and you've dragged the box of Christmas decorations out of storage and opened it, only to find that its contents look distinctly battered, tatty and sad, where once they were sparkling, bright and cheerful. So it's time to inject some new festive spirit into your seasonal display, and what better way to do that than by plundering your winter garden?

Simple, dried teasels, pine cones and poppy seedheads make charming natural Christmas decorations, but they also look wonderful when sprayed and decorated. So make the most of your winter garden and collect up any spent blooms or seedheads that will make good decorations. Leave them in a warm room to dry off thoroughly, then spray them with gold paint. When the paint is dry, attach small beads using thin florist's wire, then hang up the finished decorations on pieces of narrow, coloured ribbon for a rich, elegant effect.

TIP
These decorations are so light that you can hang them from thin birch branches or sticks of willow and twisted hazel, instead of a traditional Christmas tree.

Make a Christmas heart

When to do it: December

You will need:

- Evergreen foliage and pine cones
- Secateurs
- Galvanised mesh panel, 60 x 90cm (2 x 3ft)
- Paper heart-shaped template
- Wire cutters
- 2 blocks of florist's foam 23 x 11 x 8 cm (9 x 4 x 3in)
- Florist's wire
- Hessian ribbon or coloured ribbons
- Scissors

Put your heart into Christmas with this pretty alternative to the traditional festive wreath. Using evergreen cuttings from your garden, you can make this seasonal decoration a truly personal one.

First, get out into the garden with a pair of secateurs and gather lots of sprigs of evergreen foliage. We used rosemary, euonymus and eucalyptus, along with festive favourites such as holly, conifer foliage and cones, but you can use whatever you have to hand that would make a varied, appealing display.

To make the framework, snip the sheet of wire mesh in half using wire cutters and, with a paper template as a guide, cut out a heart from each piece of mesh. Slice the blocks of florist's foam into three, and arrange them on one of the hearts. Cut them to fit the shape, leaving a 3cm (1.25in) margin around the outside. Put the other heart on top and join the edges together – but take care as they may be sharp.

Decorate your heart by pushing the foliage sprigs into the foam until neither mesh nor foam is visible. Add a few cones, attached with florist's wire, then tie ribbon to the back of the mesh and hang the finished heart on your door.

TIP
Empty and clean the frame once the festive season is over, then store it for use again next Christmas. Alternatively, keep it handy and clad it in evergreens and roses on Valentine's Day.

Index

Picture credits

Random House and *Gardeners' World Magazine*
would like to thank the following for providing
photographs. While every effort has been made
to trace and acknowledge all photographers,
we should like to apologize should there be any
errors or omissions.

Jonathan Buckley p31; Peter Cassidy p67; Torie
Chugg p131, p133, p137, p141, p143, p145,
p147, p153; Sarah Cuttle p95; Dig Pictures/Freia
Turland p129; Paul Debois p17, p35, p41, p47,
p73, p93, p97, p99, p101, p105, p107, p109,
p111, p113, p119, p123, p125, p127, p134, p149,
p157, p181, p183, p185, p187, p189, p191, p193,
p195, p197, p199, p201, p203, p205, p207, p209;
Trish Grant p159; Stephen Hamilton p23, p39,
p25, p53, p57, p87; Caroline Hughes p177; Jason
Ingram p37, p71, p75, p77, p83, p85, p91, p117,
p151; David Murray p121, p173; Adam Pasco
p59; Vivian Russell p161; Tim Sandall p11, p13,
p15, p19, p27, p21, p33, p43, p45 p51, p61, p63,
p89, p65, p79, p81, p103, p139, p155, p163,
p167, p169, p175, p179; William Shaw p9, p29,
p49, p171; Nick Smith p55, p165; John Trenholm
p115; *Gardeners' World Magazine* p69